The End *of* Self-Help

DISCOVERING PEACE AND HAPPINESS RIGHT AT THE HEART OF YOUR MESSY, SCARY, BRILLIANT LIFE

DR. GAIL BRENNER

Ananda Press

Published by Ananda Press

The information in this book is solely for general personal use and education. It should not be treated as a substitute for professional assistance, psychotherapy, or counseling. In the event of physical or emotional distress, please consult with appropriate health care professionals. The application of information in this book is the choice of each reader, who assumes full responsibility for his or her understandings, interpretations, and results. The author assumes no responsibility for the actions or choices of any reader.

Printed in the United States of America

ISBN-13 (paperback): 978-0-9864282-0-3
ISBN-13 (ebook): 978-0-9864282-1-0

Cover design by Thomas McGee, Writely Designed
Book design by Lorie DeWorken, MIND the MARGINS, LLC
Cover photo by Kenedy Singer

*Dedicated to the possibility,
alive in you in this very moment,
of knowing that you are free.*

Contents

Introduction

Several years ago, I was speaking to my mother, sharing with her the most wonderful discovery imaginable. I described how, in any moment, anyone can know the deepest peace that's completely fulfilled and lacks nothing. I explained how this experience is always here and available, the living possibility for all of us. A flash of understanding lit up in her eyes, as she questioned, "Why doesn't everyone know this?"

I had posed the same question years earlier when I began to discover that it was truly possible to move through emotional pain and be at peace. If we don't *have to* suffer, why do we? Why don't we just know how to be okay?

Personal suffering is a reality in this human life we live. But it's not the ultimate reality, and that's what this book is about. The understanding that underlies true and lasting peace used to be reserved for Indian sages and monks on the mountaintop. *Now life is moving to bring this possibility to all of us.* It's the only thing that can bring sanity to our strained and stressed lives.

When we don't really know what to do about our pain and confusion, we do our best. And this is how the self-help movement came into being. It offers strategies and perspectives to help you find relief from suffering, but it contains a fundamental misunderstanding that, sadly, will keep you searching for happiness but not actually finding it.

With advice to love yourself more, think more positively, and remember to feel grateful, you might feel better for some time. But until you know yourself to be essentially whole, and not the wounded and broken one who needs to be fixed, the true solution to your personal suffering will remain out of reach.

What is offered here is a radical departure from conventional techniques for happiness. It directs your attention not toward an imagined better self you hope to become, but right here to realize that peace is possible in any moment no matter what the content of your thoughts and feelings. It's the absolute truth that's been so easily overlooked.

> *" Until you know yourself to be essentially whole, the true solution to your personal suffering will remain out of reach."*

My Story

My interest in suffering and the end of suffering is long standing. Like you, I just wanted to be happy. I put together a functional life of work and friends, but I was continually plagued by anxiety, confusion, and relationship troubles. I tried the mainstream route of psychotherapy—fifteen years of it—but very little changed in the way I felt or the choices I made in my life. I even became a clinical psychologist, studying happiness and offering a healing space for others, and still I suffered.

Just feeling better wasn't enough for me. When I read in ancient spiritual teachings that enduring peace was possible, I believed it at the core of my being. I didn't know how to find this peace, but something in me said, "Yes!" I was absolutely on fire to know it in my own experience.

The search took me to Buddhist meditation retreats and the most lovely and helpful teachers. I learned to watch thoughts and feelings pass through my awareness without getting involved with them. I became more peaceful as I realized I had a choice about whether or not I engaged with a habit. And I was amazed to discover that the beliefs I held onto so strongly about myself and others weren't absolutely true. I saw how hard I was working to keep my life going and started to question my ideas about who I was and how I wanted to live in the world.

My journey left no stone unturned. Near the beginning, I spent a 10-day silent meditation retreat in tears that felt like I was crying out lifetimes of sadness and grief. Meditation offered relief from the confusion of feelings, as I learned to allow them to be without acting on them, but I had burning questions about the nature of reality that kept me searching.

As my path progressed, I noticed tendencies to judge others, which came from my own inner sense of feeling inadequate. And I saw that I was afraid to let go of control, fearful of losing my hard-won sense of independence. The more I looked into my experience, with the sincere willingness to tell the truth, the more fear became apparent. So much fear had gone unnoticed!

There was a time when I would stop whenever I felt fear, close my eyes, and simply feel it. Many times during the day, I sat on my couch feeling physical tension, contracted chest and jaw muscles, and shallow breathing. As I made the space for these sensations to be, without spinning in thought or wanting to change them, sometimes they would lessen, and sometimes not. But it didn't matter—it was relaxing to finally give up the fight and just be.

It wasn't immediate, but over time, I realized I felt less stressed. I didn't worry so much about making the right decision or trying to figure everything out. I was lighter, happier, and more loving. One morning I woke up and, much to my surprise, I realized that I hadn't been anxious for quite some time.

I was feeling better, but I still wasn't completely at peace. Looking deeper, I discovered that my thoughts themselves were not the problem. Why? If you study a thought, you'll see that it's merely a temporary appearance of words. But if you pay attention to it and repeat it in your mind, it comes to life with meaning and substance. And this is the beginning of a great deal of trouble.

It was amazing to realize that if I believed the content of a thought, I was on the road to beliefs, expectations, shoulds and should nots, emotional reactions, and all the accompanying confusion. This is what I used to call "my life." But when I didn't pay attention to these thoughts, they could arise, but I remained peaceful.

In my quest for understanding, I saw that I was not my habits of worrying or needing to control, as these eventually diminished to a great degree. So who am I? I realized that everything I took myself to be was made up and temporary. My roles as woman, daughter, psychologist, or partner—they're just labels with no real substance, and they limit me. Taking them away revealed that I was somehow still here, alive and present.

I thought about all the people in my life who are important to me and imagined losing them. I looked at every single object in my home and felt into the possibility that it could all disappear. I met the end of money, relationship, career, place to live, health, and the physical body itself. What if all of it were to go? I could not find a way to not be at peace—yet I was *still* searching.

I was on my way to Europe for yet another retreat when over dinner, my friend Rupert Spira, a spiritual teacher, asked me what I was looking for by going there. I answered, "Stability in the presence that doesn't come and go." His fiery response: "Then put your attention on what doesn't come and go!"

It hit me like a lightening bolt. The stability I was traveling to Europe to find had always been here—I was too busy trying to figure out my confusion to stop and notice it. Thoughts, perceptions, physical sensations, people, my ideas about myself and others come and go—these are objects that arise and disappear. But what is stable and ever-present? The reality of being aware. It's the pure energy of life without any thing in it, the ground of being that is the true source.

With this insight, the structure of my personal self collapsed. I realized there had been an entity that I called "me" that seemed to be located as a knot in my forehead. When that contraction dissolved, there was only vast, alive space, like my head had blown open. I perceived no more barrier between me and anything else.

Around that time, I was having a conversation with a friend, and what happened was only speaking, hearing, seeing, smiling. Yes, there was the semblance of two people at a kitchen counter, but the separate forms were barely noticed, leaving the experience of pure intimacy and what I could only call love.

What a relief to realize that I didn't have to get rid of anything! I had put so much effort into quieting thoughts and eliminating painful emotions. But who was doing all this efforting? Being aware simply is and has no resistance to anything that appears. The experience of peace is indescribable. It's simply the outpouring of life in its natural state, unhindered by fears, needs, desires, and identifications.

Living this new discovery, I truly found peace and happiness right here at the heart of my messy, scary, brilliant life. I sometimes play out habits, then wake up to realize I've never left my true home. When emotions come, I experience them fully. It's life bringing me just what is needed to allow me to open again and again.

And now I live a normal life. But what is ordinary on the surface is absolutely extraordinary. The deepest peace…a heart overflowing…complete acceptance of things as they are…clear seeing that simplifies choices…unwavering willingness to not move when things get hard. It's love in motion.

Back to You

This process of investigating how you make yourself limited and discovering your true identity is not for the faint of heart. If you are less than completely open, you'll travel a rocky road. You must be willing to question everything and to lose all you hold dear. There is no reason to embark on this investigation other than because you feel moved to.

Yes, I was motivated to find an end to suffering—and discovered it. But that is an understanding from the limited, personal perspective. Looking through the eyes of universal awareness, things just happen, and who is to say why. I'm overcome by the grace of it all.

So why read this book, go to retreats, or investigate the nature of reality? If you've read this far, I'm assuming that you want to be free. You want an end to your suffering, you want to know the absolute truth, and you somehow think that this is possible for you. It is.

You're about to travel a pathless path—pathless because it goes nowhere but to the realization of being here now, awake and alive. You don't become anything. You simply recognize what you've overlooked in your experience—and it's available now.

A path this revolutionary requires guidance, and that's why I've written

" You're about to travel a pathless path— pathless because it goes nowhere but to the realization of being here now, awake and alive."

this book. It offers a bridge between the common psychological problems people experience and the true spiritual understanding that sets you free. The mind is a force to be reckoned with, and familiar habits can keep you looking out at the world through a very murky window. Together we'll meticulously explore how you get stuck in unhappiness and how to discover that the peace you long for is always available right here, right now.

We'll unravel how you're held back by your past and paralyzed by your worries about the future. You'll learn how to study fear, sadness, shame, and all your emotions so they no longer define you. And you'll begin to tap into the well of infinite potential once you know you're not a separate, damaged, and limited self. All along, I offer reflections, experiments, and guided meditations (available online at www.GailBrenner.com/books) that support you in realizing and living daily life in the deepest peace and acceptance.

Even though you may be living with your attention out in a worldly life of work and family, your true home is and always has been here. As an important stepping stone to realizing this, you'll learn how to recognize patterns of thinking and behavior you play out in your life and how to stop running from your feelings and welcome them instead. There is a good chance you'll feel happier and your life situation will improve. But there's more. And this is why what's offered here goes well beyond the popular suggestion to be mindful of your experience.

If you want to be completely free, stay with the investigation until you know who you are. You are not anything your thoughts tell you that you are. You're not your emotions or attachments to people and things. You're not your habits, addictions, or personality traits. Or even a person with a body. Anything that comes and goes is not real and is not you. You are aware, alive to each moment, and as awareness, you've never not been here.

In our study together, I invite you to take it slowly. The most important quality to bring to this journey is openness—to everything. Don't believe what you read, but let it inspire you to question your own experience. Don't take anything for granted. Keep looking within to see what is actually true for you.

Although the inquiry into who you are can be serious business, keep it light as well. Your true nature is closer than you could ever imagine, and the signs of it are everywhere. Recognize moments of peace and happiness, and experience them deeply. Let yourself be awed by beauty in all forms. Notice when you're spontaneously joyful or lost in the flow of an engaging experience. Feel the depths of love. These are moments of pure being, and you can learn from them when you're bogged down by fear, need, lack, or desire.

Here is my best attempt to explain what can only be known directly and to put words to that which can never be spoken. May your journey home be fruitful.

Always in love,
Gail
November 2014
Santa Barbara, CA

1

Finding Yourself

The self-help industry is fundamentally flawed. It perpetuates the myth that we are limited, damaged, inadequate selves who need to be fixed. Sadly, it keeps millions of people just like you hoping for a better future when they will finally be happy and fulfilled.

But what if this inadequate self isn't who you are? What if it's possible, at any moment, to be happy and free?

Discovering this possibility is a journey that leads you to the amazing fact that all you seek has always been here. What you discover won't be new or unfamiliar. *You've always been who you really are, despite your distractions.*

- You've already delighted in the burst of joy that comes out of nowhere, if only for an instant;
- You've felt the all-consuming feeling of love;
- You know the wondrous sense of the unity of all;
- You've experienced the spark of unexpected creative expression, and
- You've dissolved into a bout of uncontrollable laughter.

You know in your heart of hearts that you're bigger than your imagined limits.

Happiness isn't nearly as elusive as you might think—if you know where to look for it. There's a current alive in each of us that flows toward contentment, toward resting effortlessly in peace and ease. This current is so strong that every action we take is an attempt to find happiness.

When you seek approval, you're trying to feel whole and relaxed. If you strive for money or material goods, you're searching for the moment of ease when you finally fulfill your desire. If you overdo anything, you're really looking for happiness, peace, and relief from inner turmoil.

You might think you want a relationship or the perfect job or even your mother's love. But, your real desire is the inner longing to be free of conflict, satisfied and complete, with no sense of something missing.

This is the ease of being you've been searching for your whole life. And you absolutely *can* know it in your own direct experience.

But you won't discover it in the objects, people, and situations in the world. You won't even discover it in your own thoughts. These are changeable, unreliable forms you can't trust to make or keep you happy. If this is where you're looking, then you probably already know your search will fail.

> *" The good news — the most amazing news — is that the peace you long for is available, here and now, in this very moment."*

The good news—the most amazing news—is that the peace you long for is available, here and now, in this very moment…and endlessly. You come to know it when you learn how to stop relying on ideas about how you wish things were—and say "Yes!" to the reality of how things actually are.

The path to realizing the unlimited potential for happiness in every moment is radical. It involves a shift in consciousness that invites you to question everything you take to be true—all the stories, beliefs, hopes, expectations, and feelings that make up who you think you are—and discover that they're the very source of your dissatisfaction, unhappiness, and personal suffering.

Take an honest look at the thoughts and feelings that consume your attention. Are you:

- Waiting for others to do something so you can be happy?

- Obsessing over all the things you don't like about yourself?

- Recycling thoughts about what should or shouldn't happen in your life?

- Living in fear, shame, worry, or depression?

No wonder you're not happy. These everyday problems set you up for frustration and disappointment. They make you think the present is unfulfilling, and they delude you into believing that the ease you seek will be available at some future time. This "if only" thinking keeps you chasing happiness rather than living it. And while you're distracted by these thoughts and feelings, the deepest peace and happiness—available *right now*—go unnoticed.

Let me be clear: we're not just talking about that smile-on-your-face feeling we call happiness. It's not even the satisfaction you feel when things are going well—these are *expressions* of it.

When you deeply accept everything as it is, the inner war with your own experience ends, and you're not only peaceful, but joyful and content, as well. This is your natural state: what you knew before any conditioned habits or emotional pain concealed it. It's the pure aliveness that remains—when the pressure to do, fix, try, and accomplish falls away. Fear subsides, and you feel intimately connected with everything.

This is the happiness that is always available, always ready to be discovered. Even though you may not consciously experience it, you and I both know that it's here. Even if it's hidden, this loving presence is alive in your true heart.

Coming Home to Now

You're right to want happiness. But too often you look for it in the wrong places. With your best intentions—and using a colorful array of strategies—you constantly search for a sense of well being. But this very activity distracts you from what you seek.

There's a purity in everything that happens. But then you personalize it by analyzing, overthinking, worrying, ruminating, and endlessly discussing your problems. To feel safe, you try to change your thoughts, change your ideas about the past, and control the future. You orient your life around obtaining approval, love, and recognition because you want to finally feel whole. And when you don't find that wholeness, you eat, drink, get high, text, and stay ridiculously busy—anything for some momentary relief from your troubled emotions.

When you look outside yourself, you find that even satisfying relationships, material objects, and positive circumstances don't last. Something eventually changes—and it might be your enjoyment of them. Have you ever loved receiving a new possession only to lose interest in it later on? You won't find happiness in these fleeting things you can't control.

These exhausting attempts to be happy feel to most of us like normal life—a lot of trying without truly being fulfilled. But actually, this is *resisting* life—fixating on problems, or on escaping them. All the struggling to locate this sense of ease somewhere else—in pleasant thoughts and feelings or more positive life circumstances—has kept you from realizing the miracle that you can live it in this "now" moment.

Isn't this exactly what you've been longing for?

The Power of Attention

If the peace you seek is available now, why don't you know it? To answer this question, let's investigate the most powerful force you control and your best ally—your attention. A lot of your attention is consumed by thinking. Thoughts lure you in to think them, believe them, and make them seem absolutely real. They tell stories that create worries about the future and regrets about the past. They make you hope, search, desire, judge, fantasize, and assume.

And what about emotions? If you pay attention to emotions, they pull you into dramas, fill you with a sense of inadequacy, dread, or despair, and lead you to make choices that lack clarity and intelligence. You walk through life with unhappy feelings casting shadows on your everyday reality.

These patterns of thinking and feeling are highly conditioned—you've probably been repeating them for decades. When they take up your attention, they seem so real that you don't even consider that there may be other aspects to your reality. If you feel sad about an event from your past, for example, the story of what happened and your emotional response to it are what seem completely real to you. And you suffer.

But I'm inviting you to focus your attention elsewhere—beyond the content of thoughts and feelings. And the place to look is right at the heart of your direct experience. You're an expert at paying attention to the stories and dramas in your life. *But when your attention is glued there, it misses the simple fact of being aware.*

The alternative is this: when attention unglues from thoughts, feelings, or any other object, it rests in itself—pure awareness—and you're at peace. This is the ground of being that is always here and unchanging—no matter what appears. It's what you consciously realize when your attention no longer gets caught up in draining mental and emotional habits.

Who Are You?

As unbelievable as it may sound, this pure awareness *is* who you are, and when you know this, you're happy. *Unhappiness is merely a case of mistaken identity.* What you believe to be you is a congealed mass of mostly distorted thoughts and feelings, habits and reactions. This idea of you is not absolutely real— and it's always going to feel incomplete. You *think* you're the one with this less-than-perfect life, waiting for things to change so you can finally feel okay, waiting for the time when you can stop struggling to be better than you are. If you're not happy, this is how you identify yourself—whether you realize it or not.

But what if you're not this anxious, dissatisfied person? Your true identity is not an individual with a name, a body, a past, emotions, and beliefs about yourself and the world. This is the story *about* you, but not who you actually are.

While you've been busy with your attention captured by feelings and thinking of yourself as separate and limited, you've missed the absolute truth: you have always been all that you ever wanted. Knowing yourself as pure awareness—the life force that perceives but is unchanged by what occurs—you're completely fulfilled, lacking nothing, infinite beyond imagination. You are radiant, pure, and transparent, encompassing everything, excluding nothing. By your very nature, you're completely at peace, even if difficult experiences arise.

> " *While you've been busy with your attention captured by feelings and thinking of yourself as separate and limited, you've missed the absolute truth: you have always been all that you ever wanted.* "

Worry? Self-judgment? Loneliness? Jealousy? Discontent? Betrayal? These thoughts and feelings arise for a time in the totality of you—but have nothing to do with who you really are.

Living this understanding is the revolution that changes everything, while at the same time seemingly changing nothing. This shift of attention to being aware doesn't alter the outward appearance of the world, but it unveils endless depths of peace and clarity. You realize that you're one with everything. You see the conditioned tendencies and repetitive story lines, but you know they aren't actually you so they no longer trap you.

When you know you are presence—the simplicity of being aware, rather than the complexity and confusion of what you're aware of—problems lose their impact. You're happy and at peace, taking nothing personally. Here, nothing needs to be changed or improved. Without doing anything, you are alert, awake, completely at peace, and problem-free.

The Perfect Starting Point

By now, you're probably asking, "Sounds good, but how do I get there?" And that's what this book is about. We're so used to thinking as the way to solve problems. That's fine if you want to build a skyscraper or figure out how to drive to a new destination. But thinking doesn't work in this case because the happiness you're searching for is already here before thoughts appear. You have to *look outside your mind*. And from the perspective of the mind-driven person you believe yourself to be, this is a profound shift.

What's needed is to stop doing anything to search for happiness outside yourself so there's space to experience happiness now. How do you stop searching? "You" can't. *The search ends when the idea of you as a personal self who believes she needs to do something to be happy is seen to be false.*

The belief that we're separate leaves us living with a great deal of confusion. We assume thoughts are true when they aren't.

We strive to improve ourselves even though we never achieve our goals. We let fear guide our choices without even knowing what fear actually is. We hope to get what we want then feel disappointed when we don't. Time after time, we blindly march along, stuck in the rut of our conditioning. And we never stop to question these unsatisfying habits.

The aim of this book is two-fold: to clear up these areas of confusion and to illuminate the ever-present truth of peaceful, aware presence. Our inquiry is laser-focused as we investigate exactly what's making you unhappy so you can revel in the reality of true happiness. With a merciful heart, you'll feel the pain of living in fear and separation, and together we'll discover another way.

The starting place for our investigation is right here, with whatever you're aware of in any moment. I'll walk with you as we explore how common tendencies such as feelings of inadequacy or the need to be in control hijack your happiness. We'll examine fear, guilt, shame, grief, and resentment to shed light on the nature of stories and emotions. We'll investigate the tentacles of conditioning that live in the body.

We'll invite fundamental questions, such as:

- What is the effect of holding onto a story?

- What do I believe? Are these beliefs true?

- What exactly is this feeling that I give so much importance to?

- Who am I?

And we'll keep asking questions until all concepts lose their power to define who you are. You'll realize that letting go of what you think you are releases your awareness into the truth of who you really are. You'll glimpse the simple delight of having no resistance to life's unfolding. You'll effortlessly experience enthusiasm, uncaused joy, and simple appreciation.

And you'll recognize this potential was here, all along. *You were just too tangled up in distorted thinking and messy emotions to see it.*

Living the Yes! to Life

Denying our reality is so programmed in us that we've lost touch with the ability to say "Yes!" to life. We're masters at how to resist—which means we know how to suffer. If you believe your negative thoughts, and take your feelings as accurate barometers of your inner state, you're fighting against what's actually true. How do you know? You encounter edges everywhere.

If you think, "He shouldn't have said that," you believe your expectation about what he should have said and resist what he actually said. If you continue your career as an employee while brushing aside your passion for starting your own business, you're running on fear, resistant to the natural movement of being. If you agonize about a sad story that says you're not good enough, you're resisting the truth of your magnificence.

If you experience any conflict whatsoever, look for unexamined attachments to thoughts and feelings that have grabbed your attention. For the moment, you've forgotten who you are.

When you live in the Yes! to what is, you know that you are timeless presence where nothing is separate from anything else. You melt into the deepest acceptance of things as they are. "Not this" yields to, "Oh, this," fear dissolves into love. Emotional reactions lose their charge, along with ideas about how your life should be. With no resistance, you are one with truth and truly happy. The mind-constructed, fear-based life comes to an end, and surrendered living begins, emanating from presence. You fully embrace your human life, while flowing with things as they are.

To realize this presence, nothing needs to be destroyed or gotten rid of. This book is not about changing your inner psychology or resolving your feelings about the past, as those are temporary fixes at best. You don't need to think more positively, believe affirmations, figure out your feelings, fix yourself, manifest your desires, or become a better person. These take so much effort!

The realization of your true nature ends self-help or personal development. Why? Because there is no self to help or person to develop. It involves something much simpler: the discovery that you're not the separate entity you think you are. Here is where peace lies.

How do you come to know this way of being? Go beyond the unsatisfying objects we call thoughts and feelings to explore what else is present in your conscious experience. Then you get to experiment with living true—maybe starting right now: How do you meet your loved ones, freshly and intimately, with no scars from your history together? What about all those things you thought were so vital to accomplish? How is it to live without angst, needs, and problems? What *is* your true life purpose?

Miraculously, you have a fresh perspective on habits and situations that felt stuck, although nothing has changed except your identification with thoughts and feelings. The loving response—*not* one based on fear and separation—becomes obvious.

If you have any doubt in your mind, know this: you can realize peace. If you're struggling, you've misidentified yourself as someone you're not. Clarity is so close—it takes no

> *"Miraculously, you have a fresh perspective on habits and situations that felt stuck, although nothing has changed except your identification with thoughts and feelings."*

time at all for a simple shift of attention to being aware. Here you unveil the in-the-moment direct experience of you: clear and awake. You're home.

Walking the Path

Like a fish searching for water, you're looking to discover what's already here, and, in that sense, nothing needs to be done. But you're being asked to see beyond strongly programmed habits, so what you bring to this exploration matters. Can you be profoundly honest with yourself about what isn't working for you? Can you harness that unhappiness so you're available to a new way of being?

It serves to be totally fed up with your suffering. But have compassion as the mechanisms of conditioned habits are exposed. Be completely open in your mind, heart, and body.

In the pages of this book, you're invited to shed the light of awareness on habits you mindlessly play out in your life and to recognize those moments of pure being that we often take for granted or overlook. At the end of each chapter, you'll find reflections, experiments, investigations, and meditations that guide you to explore your in-the-moment experience. The more you work with them, the better. You can read all about the possibility of knowing your true nature—but until you step off the sidelines and into the Yes, you won't find that elusive peace and happiness. It was a light bulb moment for me when I stopped passively listening to what others were telling me about discovering peace and began to intentionally live it in my moment-to-moment experience. This changed everything for me.

Fortunately, you have a portable laboratory with you at all times to support your exploration: your own direct experience. At any moment, you can ask your inner scientist what's making you feel stuck. As you become an expert in spotting how you get trapped into suffering, you realize that infinite possibilities have always been available. Eventually, the mind gives way, and all is revealed.

What do you have to lose? See through the false, distorted, limited view of reality. Recognize your translucent, wondrous self, so fresh and alive, shining everywhere.

Explorations

1. Become familiar with your attention. Think a thought for a moment, then focus on taking a breath. Now move your attention to the sensation of your back against your chair. Notice how you can pay attention to different aspects of your experience.

   Listen to the guided audio meditation at
   www.GailBrenner.com/books.

2. Try this experiment to just see what happens—you don't have to be absolutely sure of the answer. When you see an object, are you aware? When you hear a sound, are you aware? Do you need to be focusing on something in order to be aware?

3. Think of something, anything, that brings you joy. Now stop focusing on that thing and just experience the joy itself.

4. Take some time to reflect and maybe write a list: What are the ways you say "No" to life?

2

Clear Seeing About Unhappiness

Who you are at your core is aware, alive, completely fresh, and entirely at peace—and this has always been so. This is what's so miraculous! Although you may not yet be aware of it, you're pure and innocent, untouched, not in resistance to anything—no matter how painful, shocking, or distressing your life was or continues to be.

So, if this is true, why do you feel unhappy?

This chapter lays the foundation for understanding the path to knowing your true nature. It spells out how and why we suffer and offers an overview of the way out of suffering. This is the investigation that will guide you to deconstruct—and ultimately find freedom from—the problems you perceive that erode happiness.

If it seems like a lot of information, don't be concerned. The chapters that follow will break it all down so that you can absorb it step by step.

I've intentionally repeated the ideas a few times. Often people need to hear the guidance over and over before the web of the known breaks open, offering space for a new, fresh way of being. Discovering the true "Yes!" in any moment requires a complete shift in your understanding of the nature of reality. It goes beyond any familiar philosophy, belief system, or thought process.

"Discovering the true 'Yes!' in any moment requires a complete shift in your understanding of the nature of reality."

It took me years before the clouds began to part, and looking back I appreciate having heard the same words again and again until I experienced what they were pointing to. *My goal here is be so clear, direct, and comprehensive that your mind releases its grip, making you available to the deepest peace beyond imagination.*

Now, let's get to it.

Habits and How You Define Yourself

When you lose touch with the freedom and openness of pure being, personal suffering takes center stage. It starts when you define yourself as a person with feelings and a life story who relates to other people with their feelings and life stories. If this is your reality, you'll undoubtedly feel dissatisfied and lacking.

Do any of these ring a bell?

- You repeat dramatic, emotion-laden stories in your mind.

- Your inner critic is alive and well.

- You're still plagued by what happened in your past.

- You feel anxious, fearful, or depressed.

- You orient your life around getting approval and acceptance from others.

- You worry about not being good enough.

- You distract yourself with compulsions and addictions.

- You feel like something's missing—in yourself and your relationships.

Habits like these grab on so tightly that they seem absolutely real. After all, isn't this how you behave in your life? Isn't this how you feel?

These patterns bring struggle and confusion to your life experience because you haven't stopped to investigate them—and you've mistakenly taken them to be your identity. Mindlessly putting them on day after day like your favorite pair of slippers, you experience the unsatisfying effects on you and everyone around you. In your heart of hearts, you know that peace is possible, but you can't seem to find your way there.

Where to Look for Peace

Unhappiness has nothing to do with the external situations in your life and everything to do with how you react—and how you relate to your inner reactions. Say your partner snaps at you. You might immediately respond, "I didn't do anything wrong. You have no right to treat me that way." You feel angry and frustrated, and if you bring your attention into your body, you'll notice tension and agitation. You've been triggered, and your reaction causes you to suffer.

But any time you're suffering, you have a liberating choice about what to do next. You can blame the situation, yourself, God, bad luck, your partner, and stay attached to your expectations about what he should or shouldn't do—or you can be curious about your inner experience. In the first option, you ignore or avoid your emotional reaction and instead get lost in a whirlwind of thoughts about it. "He shouldn't have... I deserve... Why me?" This prolongs your suffering because you remain trapped in the story of what happened.

The second option opens the doorway to freedom. It's revolutionary because it invites you to let go of engaging in the story so you can investigate what's actually going on inside you—the thoughts, feelings, and sensations in your body. This investigation stops the pattern in its tracks because you're relating to it in a completely new way. You're moving with the reality of what's happening rather than resisting it.

Think of your attention like food. The more you feed agitating thoughts, the more uncomfortable you feel. You might start by thinking that your partner shouldn't have snapped at you. And before you know it, your mind is complaining about every seeming infraction he's ever committed; you feel depressed and hopeless, and your whole day takes a downward spiral. You might even retort back, which complicates matters even further. This is not a happy situation, and it leaves you feeling like a victim.

The alternative is to lose interest in the story of what happened and become aware of your in-the-moment experience. As you stop feeding the content of the thoughts in your mind, you notice feelings, and you let them be present. You're aware of sensations in your body, and you simply allow them to be as they are.

But what does this have to do with happiness? Let these experiences be—without avoiding, justifying, analyzing, or ignoring them—and the troubling thoughts and feelings begin to lose their power over you. You see them as just experiences that arise and pass on. Then, as you explore the experience of being aware, you'll notice that thoughts and feelings seem to appear in awareness. What an insight! Where before you were consumed by the monologue in your head and your emotions, now there is newfound space. This experience of being aware is free, unglued from the content of these distressing objects.

You see that you don't *have to* be angry or sad, you don't *have to* be caught in an anxious or unhappy story. You realize the possibility of being peaceful and maybe even responding to the situation in new ways—once the attachment to these thoughts and feelings dissipates. You're amazed to see that this possibility has always been here, even while your attention was gripped by the drama of what happened.

Let's take another example: the need to feel accepted by others. If you experience this need, your internal world will certainly be stressful with thoughts swirling in your mind telling you you're unworthy or flawed. You live in the hope that others will approve of you—but you have a sneaking suspicion they won't. And you hesitate to express your opinions or say "no" to people's requests of you. Trying so hard to please others, you're likely to feel sad, lonely, tired, and even taken advantage of.

Some of us—maybe you—live with this constellation of inner experiences for decades. This very uncomfortable way of thinking, feeling, and behaving seems so legitimate. And you feel powerless to do anything about it. Is this the best that life has to offer?

Thankfully, you do have a choice. You can continue to resist by inhabiting the character of the you who is unworthy, hoping your distress will eventually subside. Or you can pause the story playing in your mind and discover your actual experience: feelings and physical sensations arising in awareness. This is the opening into meeting yourself as you are. In any given moment, if you're not adding fuel to the story that something's missing, you're just here as presence, with thoughts, feelings, and physical sensations arising. From this understanding of what's true, where's the problem?

It may take time for this pattern to unwind because the mind tends to hold on tightly. But each time you wake up to realize that you can rest as awareness and not play out the old story— again, your identity that was limited by the story unravels just a little bit more. Each time is a glimpse into the freedom that is possible when you know who you are.

The return home to yourself, where peace is your abiding experience and joy can't help but bubble over, asks you to stop looking outside yourself for solutions. You'll reach a turning point when you stop blaming others for your problems or waiting for the right life circumstances to bring you happiness and fulfillment. Think of it as making a U-turn with your attention toward yourself. No matter what events happen, here you are, aware of it all. You're the awareness experiencing thoughts, feelings, and physical sensations—without reacting to them. These are moments filled with grace.

Separation Is the Fundamental Misunderstanding

Where do these tendencies come from—the ones that bring unhappiness and disharmony to your life? Without realizing it, you learned them over the course of your life experience, and they grabbed your attention so much that you couldn't let them go. Relentlessly reinforced, they came to define you, your life, and your world, while masking your natural state of ease and peace. Mistakenly believing yourself to be a separate and limited person, you've disconnected from the truth of your being.

Separation, though, is not the enemy. It's a natural developmental process that's all about survival in the human world. As an infant, you start out experiencing reality as undivided. There's no "you" and "other"—everything is the same, undifferentiated from your experience of it.

Then, in just a few months, you begin to perceive that you're separate from the things and people around you. Now, there's a "you," other people, and separate objects. This amazing development enables you to learn how to function in the world, get your needs met, and play and grow. Young children are infinitely curious about how they relate to that fascinating world of people and objects out there. Yet, this is also the beginning of forgetting your true identity.

You start believing what others tell you: that who you are is defined by your name, relationships, history, needs, ideas, feelings, and accomplishments. You assume that what you have and don't have describes you. You lose touch with the natural sense of pure being that pervades everything, instead feeling trapped in mental ideas about yourself and everything else. This is separation.

Virtually nothing about our world reminds us of who we actually are. Our lives take place in the context of institutions— families, schools, governments, businesses—and the stories that make them seem so real. Caught in the collective trance of mistaken identity that divides and separates, we're trained to inhabit a mind-created reality. But we never stop to consider that this isn't how things actually are.

But here's a potent sign that something is off in your understanding of reality: you suffer. Yes, you may experience times of contentment when circumstances make you feel happy and fulfilled. But later, you're dissatisfied once again. Eventually, you wonder, 'is this all there is in life? Am I ever going to be truly happy?'

Further fortifying your belief in separation is the pain you hold from unresolved events in your past. As children, when we feel threatened—by abandonment, neglect, criticism, abuse, lack of love, pressure to meet our parents' expectations—we scramble to somehow figure out how to cope. This is the natural human response to anxiety and confusion. Trying desperately to restore a sense of safety and well being, we developed distorted belief

" Without an intelligent, foolproof approach to ending the pain of the past, these failed strategies—and the suffering they create— will stay firmly in place."

systems about ourselves and the world and patterns of relating to others that make sense when we're young, but are ultimately dysfunctional. This is how we learn that we need to protect ourselves by hiding our emotions, working to get approval, and maintaining control at all costs. Short-term, these coping behaviors were intended to help us. But you don't need me to tell you that they just don't work.

Without an intelligent, foolproof approach to ending the pain of the past, these failed strategies—and the suffering they create—will stay firmly in place. Your mind will chew on what happened, your body will react as if no time has passed, and your emotions and behavior will feel out of your control.

You've lost touch with the radiance of being. You've misidentified as limited and separate—while overlooking the possibility of peace.

A Glimpse into the End of Suffering

Conventionally, to address these problems, we spend years in psychotherapy, repeat affirmations to promote positive thinking, or read self-help books to try to untangle the past. But here we take a different tack, which is the way of truth.

The true medicine for the challenging experiences you had as a child isn't to find resolution within the story of what happened. In the end, it doesn't matter who did what to whom. You might feel like a victim of your circumstances, but that is just another identity you take on. And it doesn't help you find the clarity and peace you long for.

The past, with its intriguing stories and very sticky emotional residue, doesn't exist in the way you commonly think about it. The true meaning of the past is not in the events that occurred—it's in your reaction to them. When you look clearly, you'll see that what you call your unresolved problems from the past are actually a pattern of emotions with a strong physical component and memories that arise now, in the field of presence. When you welcome these experiences as appearances that you're aware of—rather than taking them as real, meaningful, and personal—they begin to lose their power to define you. Eventually, the deepest peace is revealed. What once loomed as a problem causes barely a ripple of disturbance in you. This is the seed of possibility alive in your heart, waiting for your kind attention.

Why You Suffer

Going deeper to the root of the habits and tendencies you play out in your life, we find undigested emotional pain, which is why you suffer. None of us consistently had all our basic needs met when we were young. And some of us were unsupported in major ways. Which of these describes you?

- You were left in your crib when you needed food or loving attention,

- You were told that some of your behavior was unacceptable, so you felt ashamed,

- Your accomplishments were ignored or you were pushed to succeed,

- You were heavily criticized—so you either vowed to prove yourself or got lost in self-doubt,

- You were the target of physical, sexual, or emotional abuse.

Children naturally have emotional reactions to frightening or confusing situations like these. All emotions begin with strong physical sensations in the body, and eventually include the label of a particular feeling, once the child is old enough to use language. For example, if an adult yelled at you when you were young, your body immediately tensed up, a natural reaction to feeling threatened. Left without a way to safely and consciously experience these sensations—and the space for you to express what you feel—you sat helplessly seething in frustration or seized up in fear.

Children are not equipped to deal with strong feelings on their own and many parents don't know how to honor their children's emotional life. Ideally, when you experienced an emotional reaction as a child, your parent would acknowledge it without judgment, which would allow the feeling to be welcomed and released. Your feeling is accepted as okay so you don't need to resist or deny it. It doesn't have to go underground, so there's no residue and you return to a state of ease.

But when adults don't have the skills to cope with their own strong feelings and therefore can't support their child in doing so, you're left with an experience that is too overwhelming and painful to bear. If your feelings are judged or ignored, you'll feel confused, threatened, and unsafe. Over time, the best way you can come up with to restore your sense of safety is to suppress the feeling and push it out of awareness. And so, we become masters at pretending feelings aren't present.

But when feelings are buried, out of conscious awareness, you experience yourself as fragmented. The effects of difficult feelings are still lodged in the body, hiding out in the darkness of unconsciousness—because they haven't been recognized and given the space and acceptance needed for release. We believe they're just too painful.

These unexplored sensations cause thoughts to swirl, as you try incessantly in your mind to make sense of your inner experience. Something doesn't feel quite right, but you just can't get to the bottom of it. When situations trigger these feelings, you experience physical tension, and your thoughts, emotions, and behavior seem out of control. You so desperately want to be happy and at peace, but you keep recycling the very behaviors that make you unhappy. You feel separate, alienated, and confused.

This undigested pain, stuck in the body as habitual contractions, leads to an array of coping strategies and behaviors that keep your feelings at bay. The results? Addiction to substances, shopping, sex, or food; avoiding conflict at all costs; pushing to get your way; seeking love and attention; perfectionism; procrastination; overworking; low self-esteem; arrogance…the list goes on. We've come up with endless ways to shield ourselves from facing difficult emotions.

At the core of these habits is the wish to be happy—but their function is to avoid pain and deny the truth of what you're actually experiencing. And they continue to frustrate you until you make that U-turn with your attention and lovingly meet what you've been running from.

When you do, take a deep breath and congratulate yourself! This is the beginning of a beautiful friendship—with your own experience. It is also the way home to the peace you long for.

Finding Your Way to Peace

Feelings that remain unexplored are at the root of the habits you play out that leave you discontented and stuck. And turning to meet your in-the-moment experience by saying, "Yes!" to it, changes everything. You see clearly the structure of these habits—how they are made up of beliefs and expectations that are at odds with reality as it actually appears. And you recognize and consciously feel the emotions that have been hidden from awareness.

Say that you're trying to complete a project but you find yourself procrastinating. Your attention gets pulled into activities that have nothing to do with what you want to accomplish, and you finish the day feeling disappointed in yourself. The next day, you might try some strategies to help you stay focused, but again find yourself distracted. You're far from being at peace.

This pattern is likely to continue until you bring your attention directly into it by noticing the thoughts and feelings you're experiencing right when they're happening. First, you become aware of thoughts:

- I failed to accomplish my goals for the day,

- I'm angry with myself,

- I worry about when I'll complete the project.

Then, moving your attention into your body, you discover a flood of physical sensations you didn't realize were present. You notice tension in the back of your neck, jitteriness in your belly, and tightness in your jaw. And it becomes obvious to you that the emotion you're experiencing is fear. While being lost in the fog of procrastinating, you've overlooked the underlying emotion, fear, and the physical sensations that are part of the fear experience.

If you're like me, this will be a surprising discovery. There are so many feelings and sensations in the body that go unnoticed, so much of the stuff of life—your precious experience—that you've been missing! And this is the doorway to happiness and peace greater than you could ever imagine. How does that work? Let's explore more deeply to discover it.

When you are aware of a sensation, say tightness in your jaw, here is what's happening: there is you being aware and there is the sensation of tightness. What is this "you being aware" like, apart from the tightness you are aware of? If you put your attention on being aware, you'll notice some things about it. It's open, friendly, benign, neutral but welcoming, and it emanates a sense of being okay. It doesn't push or pull. It has no boundaries, no line of demarcation that separates it from anything. It's here and everywhere; it just is.

Resting in this awareness, you might feel relaxed and less tied up in knots. And, if you look closely, you'll see that you can just be aware without always having your attention attached to something you're aware of.

Why don't you do the experiment right now? After you read the rest of this paragraph, put the book down and be aware of any physical sensation that's appearing right now. Then shift your attention away from the sensation and to the awareness, "you being aware." Stay here for a minute or two. What is your experience?

What's absolutely true is that you are now and always have been aware. You know the experience of being aware of objects. You're aware of the things around you, when you're interacting with someone and each of you is speaking, when you think, feel, move, or experience hunger. You may not have realized it, but awareness has been present at the heart of every experience you've ever had. If it hadn't been, there's no way you could have known that something happened.

And you now know from your own experiment that you are aware, whether or not you're aware of any objects. This is pure being, and it's peaceful and free of conflict. Objects like sensations, thoughts, or feelings can arise and dissolve in awareness. But awareness, that stable, spacious, easeful state, is ever-present.

Just like the space in a room filled with furniture, awareness has no problem with anything that arises in it. It is infinitely capable of welcoming emotional pain—the hurt, anger, terror, lack, and anything else you've been suppressing for so long.

Whatever you've been defending against, avoiding, or hiding from—no matter how distasteful or scary it is—can finally come out of the shadows of your heart, mind, body, and spirit because you are now intimately aware of the space that can hold it all.

Each time your attention rests as awareness, you stop interfering with the flow of life. Everything can be as it is without needing to protect yourself from it. You can simply be as experience unfolds. You'll find it relaxing because you're no longer working to keep your feelings at bay.

And here's what's amazing: you always have a choice in every single moment, and it's the essential choice that will set you free. You can keep your attention engrossed with traumatic stories about what happened in the past, worries about the future, and negative judgments about yourself and the world. Or you can shift your attention to awareness and be free.

You can identify yourself as the separate and limited person who always feels that something's missing. Or you can live as awareness, which is the pure essence of life itself. Here your perspective shifts from fear-based activities that attempt to protect and fix to the wisdom of meeting things as they are. You move from hope for a better future to a deep and lovely acceptance of all that's here now.

This is the beautiful, sacred choice that is yours in any moment.

By now, the patterns and habits you created to hide from your feelings are strongly conditioned. It's like you've been walking back and forth along the same five-foot stretch of ground for decades, and you're dug in deep. You feel lost in these habits, playing them out automatically and feeling like they control you. And the possibility of living as pure awareness seems a million miles away.

This is the perfect starting point! Simply take any moment, and be aware of your right now experience.

- What are you feeling?

- What thoughts are appearing?

- What sensations are you aware of?

And what is all of this appearing in? You can discover in any moment that you are aware and rest your attention here. This allows the structure of your habits to unwind and you start to see that there is another way to be. A way that is conscious, alive, and at peace.

It's like taking the wind out of the sails of these habits. Once you see them as they are—not as the drama and struggle that they seemed to be—they begin to lose their power to grab you and pull you into suffering.

Welcoming your in-the-moment experience reveals some amazing insights. There are no wounds inside of you and no inner child to be healed. What you actually find are thought patterns, feelings, and sensations arising in presence. Even though you might feel damaged, you—pure being that is infinitely open and endlessly spacious—have never been the least bit touched by anything that has ever happened. So there's nothing to repair or improve. The way out of unhappiness is actually quite simple, much simpler than most therapists or self-help books will lead you

" Welcoming your in-the-moment experience reveals some amazing insights. There are no wounds inside of you and no inner child to be healed."

to believe: You make a commitment, in every moment of suffering, to turn your attention directly into yourself and away from the distractions of your confusing stories and agitating feelings. Here you discover pure awareness, alive and undisturbed.

That said, the stories and feelings you experience may be woven so deeply into your mind and body that they keep a very tight grip. Unwinding the power of the story and liberating the feelings in your body takes gentle ongoing attention for many of us. It may help to write about what happened with the intention of finally releasing the story so you can focus on your direct experience of sensations in the body. You might also consider working for a time with a psychotherapist, *but only one who understands that healing isn't found within the story.* Always return to your true nature as pure being to support your recognition of peace.

Let this understanding of how unhappiness works saturate your struggles and problems. Begin to question everything you take to be true and unchanging about yourself, others, and the world. Lift the veils that obscure your clear vision and sense the perfume of presence.

Effortless Being

These habitual ways of thinking, feeling, and behaving are long lasting. For most of us, it takes time to wind down the momentum of these patterns. As you refrain from feeding them with meaning and importance as much as you can, they gradually cease to affect you. You recognize that you are not disturbed by them. You more often return back to yourself and begin to live as the peace that you are. Like me, you may wake up one morning and realize that you haven't felt anxious for quite some time. It feels like a miracle.

But here's the paradox—and it's the essential point that will set you free. It's natural to want to feel better. But if you're attached to outcomes—such as relief or peace or specific changes in your behavior or life circumstances—you're embodying a belief that there's someone who experiences them or causes them to happen. You're still wanting something you think isn't here right now.

The invitation is to return back to yourself, to remember who you are, to reveal what has always been true, which is that you are not a limited, separate self. You are awareness—undivided, excluding nothing, the source of life that animates everything. This is what you discover when the fascination with conditioned habits wanes, and you consciously know reality as it already is. This shift isn't about improving yourself or fixing what you think is broken about you. Instead, you realize that there's no entity that is you who needs to be improved and that you have never *not* been whole.

Rather than seeking to be different than you are right now, explore the truth of your in-the-moment experience. Rather than trying to improve, discover the nature of the one who thinks she's not okay as is. Be open to the being before the doing, to knowing yourself as that which is aware, prior to any objects or any suffering.

Put in some effort to counteract the trajectory of longstanding habits—and with the collapse of the one who strives, you realize the effortlessness of pure being. And here you remain, aware and alive, never having been touched by any life circumstances. Your experience of difficult feelings may subside, but this is a joyful side effect of realizing your true nature—and not a goal.

No Resistance, No Conflict

The absolute truth of you—you being aware—is not in conflict with anything that arises. This means that any disturbing thought or emotion can appear, but the awareness in which it appears remains undisturbed. When you realize this through your own direct experience, your perceived problems will melt away. Rather than inhabiting the limited world of challenges and struggles, in any moment you can know yourself as infinitely accepting awareness in which objects arise.

Now let's go a step further. It seems that you're aware, and that objects arise in awareness. But this is *still* not the deepest truth. In reality, there is just what is occurring now…and now… and now. It's simply pure being, the flow of life.

So how do objects appear? You might be saying, "Of course, there are objects. I see the trees and buildings and streets. I have thoughts. I sometimes feel angry or sad. I can touch my head with my hand. I am real; the world is real." This is because the mind is designed to label, categorize, and describe. Before these mind functions get going, there is just reality, the pure unfolding of experience that has no separate things in it. The mind's labeling of experience creates the illusion of separate objects that appear, change, and disappear in awareness. When we believe these objects to be real, we enter the world of stories and separation—and we set ourselves up to suffer. Imagine flipping the switch that turns off *all* your thinking. Are there any objects now?

Since reality has no separate objects in it—it only *seems* to— it's never in conflict with anything. Any thought, perception, or bodily sensation can appear in you, and reality has no problem with it. The worst terror you could imagine? An outpouring of grief? Guilt, shame, jealousy, disappointment, or despair? Reality doesn't judge, fight, or avoid any of it.

In any given moment, you can experience what is happening from two different perspectives: from the view of stories, feelings, or limited ideas about people and the world—*or* from the view of reality. You already know the experience of stories and feelings; they keep you busy figuring out, avoiding, being captured in drama, and troubled. But the experience of reality is completely different. You experience it by knowing the pure essence of whatever is present.

Take any situation that makes you suffer. Subtract any think-ing *about* it, which isn't really it—and there goes the story and the label of any emotion you might be feeling. Then take away the naming of any physical sensations and the labels of "body" and "me." What remains? All that's left is pure experiencing with no separate labeled objects. This is the "is-ness" of life, and it has nothing to do with thinking; it's pure aliveness. Now, where is the problem? And where is the one who thinks there's a problem?

When we experience everything as its essence, we see that nothing is separate or different from anything else. There's only the pure experiencing of everything—which means that reality is always only experiencing itself. Everything you look at, hear, perceive, think about—including yourself—shares the same true nature: pure experiencing. That's it. Nothing else is truly real. Any emotion or burst of thoughts, seen through to its essence, is just experiencing. How can reality resist experiencing itself? It's like a tree rejecting its tree nature. Impossible. Reality just is.

Who you are is always at peace and never in resistance to anything. It's the natural state of life. But you get in trouble as soon as you add back in the mind's evaluating, criticizing, should-ing, and assuming. You've just created sad stories, ideas of what should and shouldn't happen, painful feelings you don't want to face, unfulfilled needs, and a sense of lack—and a separate person who experiences these troubles. This is the too-familiar world of resistance, struggle, and friction. You've heard of inner peace? This is inner war. Fighting your own experience is not a happy way of being.

But here's some very good news: freedom from unhappiness is possible, and nothing needs to change. You don't need to change your thoughts, process your feelings, learn to relax, or

"See clearly through to the essence of what makes you unhappy, and you'll realize that, at the core of your being, there's no conflict, resistance, or separation."

become a better person. The invitation is simply to see things clearly. See clearly through to the essence of what makes you unhappy, and you'll realize that, at the core of your being, there's no conflict, resistance, or separation. You now know peace deeper than you could ever imagine. Shine a laser on every experience that makes you suffer, and you'll always find your true nature, just being.

When you live as pure experiencing, you're happy, or at least peaceful—because you're not in resistance to anything. Love overflows—because everywhere you look, you see yourself.

What About Time?

Now, let's study time, because your exploration of unhappiness will undoubtedly have something to do with the past, present, and future.

Through the eyes of absolute reality, nothing is separate—no emotions, no stories, no people (including you), no thoughts. There's only experiencing, presence. In addition, none of this occurs in a specific time—because time is also only a concept created by the mind. Look closely and you'll see that there's no actual thing called the past or future. Do you have thoughts about the past? Those thoughts are happening now. Do you worry about the future? Your worry is occurring now. Feelings, thoughts, perceptions—they're all happening now. And "now" is not a slice of time. It's the infinite is-ness of pure being uncontained by time or space.

Reality is timeless. From the perspective of awareness, we experience all that has ever happened in the timeless now. What a miracle to realize there's no time for any objects to take form! Without the input from the mind that labels, describes, and judges—without any separate self that does, feels, or experiences anything—there is just This that is, right now. It's impossible to even give it a word—because labeling is another function of the mind. What time is it? Always now. What's present in timelessness? Only reality experiencing itself.

As you bring your attention to the ways that unhappiness arises in you, see if you can hold time lightly. You may experience a strong sense of reality about events that happened in the past, what was said or done, and their effect on you. And you may notice that you think about the future with hope, dread, or worry.

Continually remind yourself that this concept of time is illusory, and do your best to return to the simple fact of you being aware. And keep in mind this radical truth: you can't resolve the stories and events of your past by rearranging your thoughts or fixing your feelings—because there will still be a sense of you as limited, as the one who struggles to keep your fears at bay. The true release comes when you recognize that nothing has ever touched you: you're timeless, free, empty of objects, but overflowing everywhere.

Are you ready to take the pathless path back to yourself? Are you ripe to consciously know the truth that's already alive as you? In any moment, shift your attention away from objects and return to yourself: infinite…peaceful…here.

Explorations

1. Contemplate the possibility of freeing yourself from mental and emotional habits. Close your eyes for as long as you like; allow space to enter all the rigid parts of your brain. Let your mind be open like the sky.

   Your body may feel contracted by habits. Again, with your eyes closed, imagine these contractions releasing. See if your body can feel fluid, spacious, and free.

   It doesn't matter what actually happens when you do these explorations. You're simply offering yourself an invitation.

   Listen to the guided audio meditation at
   www.GailBrenner.com/books.

2. Compassion is the capacity to be loving and kind in the face of pain. It's an important ingredient as you become aware of patterns that have been stuck in you.

   Consider how you can be kind to yourself by thinking about how you are kind to others. Being kind means approaching people in a friendly manner and treating them lovingly, with care. To a child in distress, you might say something encouraging like, "I understand you're hurting. It's going to be okay." Kindness is the opposite of judging and rejecting.

Can you relate to yourself with kindness as you recognize the painful patterns that you've identified with?

3. Investigate your experience to see if you can find a past or future. Notice that all you detect are thoughts *about* the past or future. Recognize that you're always present. It's only your thoughts that make you believe there is a past or future. Experiment with this understanding as you go through the day.

3

Showing Up Ripe and Ready

By now, you're beginning to understand the depth of your conditioning and how it affects you and the people around you. These patterns consist of experiences that usually occur outside of conscious awareness. People with full-blown addictions often find themselves picking up a cigarette or ordering that next drink without even realizing it. These well-entrenched patterns are so deeply embedded in the mind and body that they happen automatically.

But you can always do the radical thing, which changes everything. You can become aware of the thoughts and feelings that drive these habits. You can stop at any moment, notice what's happening in your present moment experience, and shift your attention to pure awareness. You quickly realize that engaging in these habits and making them your reality is optional.

The Power of Conditioning

Clearly, the power of conditioning is very strong. If you're at its mercy, it drags you along in its current, taking you here and there at its will, and you feel like you've lost control over yourself and your life. There you are, stressed and frustrated.

At some point, you'll get fed up. You'll begin to question your conventional, familiar reality. And as you do, you will see the fears underlying these habits. You'll see how feelings of inadequacy have limited your expression in the world. You'll become aware that you've been living with a sense that something is wrong, missing, or lacking. And you'll become open to another way.

Now, you're finally ready to release your attachment to these patterns you've held onto for so long. When you're caught in the throes of conditioning, you unknowingly worship at the

> " *When you're caught in the throes of conditioning, you unknowingly worship at the altar of fear, limitation, and discontent.* "

altar of fear, limitation, and discontent. But stopping the movement into these patterns, and instead studying what is actually happening in the moment, ends the struggle with your experience. This is the way to realize peace and happiness.

Entering the Unknown

This shift in consciousness catapults you way outside of your comfort zone. It asks you not to identify with the ways of thinking that have been defining you for decades, not to close down into the one track of your habit that has become your "reality." It invites your mind to be so blown open that all the barriers and defenses fall away—even your definition of yourself as a limited human being.

You're entering the world of the unknown—and it will feel challenging. Who are you without these oh-so-familiar ways of being? How do you function? How do you live in the land of not knowing? What will happen? Will you be safe?

These are the questions of a mind on the precipice of a brilliant discovery—a mind starting to understand that continuing to live out these patterns won't bring you the happiness you seek—a mind beginning to open.

The Paradox of Change

Questioning everything…letting go of defenses… It might sound like you're being asked for a lot of doing and changing. But here's the paradox: nothing needs to be changed or eliminated. Your defenses, beliefs, and fears aren't wrong ways of being or mistakes to be corrected. All you need is a simple shift of attention to what you've overlooked—to see that you've always been aware. Consciousness has been glued to this idea of you as a limited, separate self. Come unglued, and you'll see awareness—clear, open, at peace—and forms appearing in awareness. Look even more precisely and you'll see that all there is is being aware now. This being-aware isn't located anywhere, doesn't have any size or shape. It's simply, profoundly, all-encompassingly, freely aware.

And another paradox: "you" don't change the thoughts, emotions, and behaviors of your habitual patterns. This would take enormous effort to sustain and usually won't work anyway. But the reality of your everyday experience may change. When you realize how much your actions have been driven by fear, the natural intelligence of your true nature is free to make another choice. When you feel in your heart how your judgments and assumptions have caused separation, you simply say, "No more," and love flourishes. When you let in the truth of how you have been treating yourself poorly, new options begin to appear.

These changes seem to occur over time, but they actually happen in the timeless now. You wake up to the ways you've been deluding yourself into believing what's not true. And you realize that these mistaken beliefs are what have fueled your suffering. As the light of clear seeing begins to show from behind the clouds, you naturally soften. The daily experiences that you've taken for granted—stress, frustration, unconscious emotional reactions—are seen with fresh eyes. There's more space for happiness and joy.

From the perspective of absolute reality, everything is always unfolding in perfect alignment with the whole of life. But if you aren't at peace, and you're interested in this sacred investigation to discover the truth of who you are, it's essential to understand how your automatic habits hijack your happiness.

Don't underestimate the power of these conditioned tendencies. Until you learn how they work, you *will* get stuck in undesirable feelings and reactions. You'll miss the experience of tension in your body along with the subtle beliefs and expectations that color your view of what's going on. Coming into this investigation lukewarm or semi-committed leaves room for the momentum of conditioning to continue. If you aren't curious about your in-the-moment experience, you'll continue to feel stuck and separate. But when you start with a burning desire to know the truth, you see all these habits with full clarity, which, over time, completely changes their capacity to affect you.

What does it mean to be on fire for the truth? How do you show up? What qualities do you bring to this investigation? This is what this chapter is about.

The exploration into, through, and beyond conditioning invites you to be fierce and receptive, tenacious and loving. Your mind will attempt to deter you every step of the way on this journey. So your desire to know the truth needs to stay strong—until you realize that you can rest in the truth that is already stronger than the force of any mindless habits.

The essential qualities that you require are right here, alive in you. Find them and return to them often. They will clear the fog of confusion and smooth the way to discover yourself, right here, whole and unendingly, joyously fulfilled.

Openness

Openness is the most vital quality that supports you in recognizing that you don't have to be attached to repetitive experiences that make you suffer. When you're open, you're willing to see everything in new and surprising ways. Openness invites you to not take anything for granted—any memory, any way of thinking, any tendency to react emotionally. It's all up for potent investigation—and you can't possibly know what you will discover. Be this open, and you'll become clear about who you're not. This is the chink in your familiar armor that begins to reveal who you really are.

In your conscious mind, you might not realize that you're already intimately familiar with the timeless unfolding of experience. It's here and always happening! Something in your experience is free of conditioning, infinitely at peace. You're just not yet aware of it. The invitation stands to take a leap of faith to discover what you don't yet consciously know.

Something in you recognizes the truth of the words you're reading here. You know in your heart of hearts that it's what you want. But it hasn't yet permeated your ongoing reality.

Openness will carry you across the threshold. Are you open to…

- Not knowing what will happen?
- Living without the filter of your mind or emotions?
- Making space to release the contractions in your body?
- Allowing your relationships and life circumstances to change—but not forcing them to?
- Having things feel fresh, unfamiliar, surprising, and new?

No one can deny the innocence that is essentially you. You and your world are born afresh in every moment. You can't know what will happen or how things will unfold. But you can know that you're not the limited, separate self. You can find the place in you that doesn't resist. You can rest here and know that all is okay.

As you explore within yourself, you may discover that you're not as open as you thought you were. You might be uncomfortable letting yourself question certain beliefs or behaviors that you hold dear. Maybe you're attached to staying constantly busy or defending your "right to be right." Perhaps you're holding onto a resentment from the past, and you believe that it will only be resolved with the apology you'll never get.

There's no rule that says you should be open. Openness is an invitation, not a requirement. In fact, these areas where you can't imagine letting go are rich for inquiry: What's your direct experience of holding on so tightly? What arises in these moments of resistance? Can you simply be aware of what is, without changing anything—not even the defensiveness or resistance?

Here's the irony: you're bringing openness to the experience of being closed. When you allow even the struggle within yourself to just be, what happens? Ease. *Let struggling struggle as you rest your attention in being aware of it.*

If you're truly open, you'll put every single thing you *think* is true on the line. And in doing so, you live in questions, not answers. You're open to not knowing anything with your mind, which leaves you available to the magnificence of aware presence overflowing with life.

Curiosity

As humans, we're naturally curious from birth—searching to know, to understand, and to make sense of ourselves and the world. Have you ever watched a baby captivated by her toes or spent time with a child asking endless "why" questions? A curious mind is one that wants to know. If you're curious, you don't take things at face value. Instead, you keep asking questions until you feel satisfied that you fully understand.

Curiosity will serve you well in your search to discover unshakeable happiness. It invites you to deconstruct the thought-emotion-behavior patterns that have been your reality. Knowing that peace is possible, you drill down to the absolute essence of your present moment experience. Over time, once the patterns start to lose their grip, you realize they don't actually define who you are. It's an amazing, freeing discovery!

A curious mind is a beautiful thing when it's focused on happiness. Take a look at your life circumstances and you'll know exactly what you're curious about. Are you interested in the dramas playing out in your life? Do you think about them with guilty pleasure? Then it's not surprising that your life feels tangled up. Do you long to achieve even though you feed your feelings of lack and inadequacy? Then you'll probably never feel satisfied with your accomplishments.

Does your attention rest in present moment awareness? Then you'll be relaxed and joyful.

Ultimately, there's no separation between the inner life and the outer world. If you focus on thoughts of stress and unhappiness, then you'll experience stress and unhappiness in your life circumstances and relationships. But if you long for abiding peace, turn your curiosity toward directly knowing the truth of your experience that's here now—and see the peace and happiness you discover reflected everywhere.

> " Ultimately, there's no separation between the inner life and the outer world."

You might think that being curious means that you find out why things are as they are. Do any of these sound familiar?

- Why did that happen to me?

- Why did I do that?

- Why didn't I do this instead?

- Why did she say that to me?

Some of us get lost in relentless questioning to understand by asking "why."

The mind can easily grab hold of these questions and chew on them forever. You may try to answer them, but the answers only take you deeper into the muck of discontent and confused thinking. Let's examine, "Why did that happen to me?" Your answers might be: because the other person shouldn't have done what they did, because I'm a loser, because I was in the wrong place at the wrong time, because I wasn't loved enough as a child. These unsatisfactory answers only breed more questions—and more discontent and confusion.

But here you're invited to channel your curiosity to shine like a laser directly on what you're experiencing in the moment. Instead of asking "why"—which traps your attention squarely in thought—try these questions, which open you to what's here right now. Instead of getting you thinking, they draw your attention from your mind into being with what is:

- What am I actually experiencing?

- What am I paying attention to that's increasing my unhappiness?

- Even though thoughts, feelings, and physical sensations are present, am I aware?

- What happens when I disengage with the thoughts and emotions that are appearing and simply rest as awareness?

- What is "being aware" like? Is it finite—or infinite?

Questions like these offer experiments that come from a place of not knowing. They open door after wondrous door, infinitely. Directed in this way, curiosity doesn't reinforce the activity of thinking, but helps you to move outside the thinking mind and explore your actual experience. Then, the opportunity for deeper research naturally arises:

- Where does my attention go if I stop feeding the "why" question?

- If I remain aware rather than engaging with the familiar objects that arise, what do I think or feel? What happens to my relationships? How do I know what to do next?

These questions take you well beyond any conventional notions of curiosity. They invite you to be infinitely open to the totality of experience—so open that even your ideas about yourself become questionable. This is where you find the release from *trying* to find happiness to actually *knowing* it. Are you really who you think you are? Laser-like questioning, starting with your experience in this moment, deconstructs the ideas and emotions you've clung to until there's nothing left to do but surrender.

Curiosity about ourselves is far from new. The phrase, "Know thyself," is etched into the ruins of a Greek temple built 2400 years ago. But how to know thyself?

Start with childlike curiosity that doesn't know, then pose questions that help you discover what's real—right here and now—like those suggested above. Don't know anything with your mind—and you will know yourself as the luminous presence of life shining everywhere.

Receptivity

There's a beautiful relaxation that happens when you're receptive. You let go of the stance of "I know." You don't need to spend your energy controlling everything. You're willing to stop trying to impact what happens and simply receive what's offered. Receptivity comes when you surrender your *attachment* to your personal traits and identities and let yourself stand unveiled, without any identity or familiar grounding in who you think you are or what you think you need to do.

With no defenses in the way, you become pure receptivity, willing to listen deeply to guidance that occurs to you, willing to feel the stickiness of your familiar habits and tendencies—even while remaining receptive. It's like listening with your heart, with every cell of your body, with the deepest place in you that trusts.

Receptivity comes when you're willing to put everything down—everything that defines you as a separate person in the world. Your repetitive thought patterns, habitual ways of suffering, perceived needs, fears and projections, the perception that your body and mind are you—anything you believe in can go. And there you are: pure, innocent, and so alive!

How do you let go to be receptive? Feel the effects of the fears that drive you—how they confuse you and limit your choices. Admit that your frustration and despair can't be fixed and that you don't know what to do. Say, "No more!" even though you don't really know where that will take you. At this crossroads, where you tell the truth and face yourself without blinders on, you're open to new possibilities.

A turning point came for me when I realized I'd been hoping for a miracle of divine intervention that would enter me and take away the pain. Like a starving baby bird straining its neck for the next worm to show up, I had been waiting to be fed the morsel of insight that would set me free. I didn't understand that I actually had to study reality to know what's true in my own experience.

It was a light bulb moment that brought the fire of receptivity. I heard what I'd heard a million times before, but in a different way. I was diligent about noticing when I felt even an iota of agitation or fear, and I refused to let this discomfort continue unexamined. For months, I spent a lot of time sitting on my couch, feeling my in-the-moment bodily experience, simply being aware while ignoring any stories running in my mind.

The coagulated energy in my cells from years of avoidance finally had room to move. And eventually, the old habits began to loosen their grip. There was now space to explore what is here once the attachment to mind- and emotion-driven tendencies diminished. My body relaxed tremendously, and I had times of realizing pure presence—a ground of peace that had been there all along. What I thought of as "me" just didn't fit anymore.

I welcomed each time I was triggered as an opportunity to be with what is. It was, and still is, joyful to simply be receptive to what's happening, fearlessly intimate with all.

You can't make yourself be receptive. It's something that happens effortlessly when the natural intelligence of life begins to infiltrate your being, which it's doing right now! But here's how to get ready:

- Tell yourself the truth about your own unhappiness, and be open to another way of being.

- Stop looking for solutions in the world and become interested in your own experience in any moment.

- Be aware that life is constantly giving you everything you need to realize freedom.

All you need to do is contemplate being receptive. How are you blocking receptivity to your own experience now? What would it be like to receive and accept things just as they are? Imagine more space in your body, mind, and heart—a body without borders, a mind open like the sky, a heart overflowing with peace.

Be receptivity itself, and you'll know yourself as the radiance of pure being.

Dedication

As we've seen, conditioned tendencies are powerful. Ask anyone who engages in any compulsive behavior—an addict, a workaholic, a rageaholic, or a people-pleaser. When caught in the trance of conditioning, you unconsciously recreate tendencies like these for years on end. These are well-entrenched grooves of mindless behavior, fueled by a distinct set of physical sensations and thought patterns that are what you call "your life." They become so familiar and real that they *almost* defy exploration.

But when you seek abiding peace, you start to question these experiences of inner conflict and confusion. If here-and-now reality couldn't possibly be in resistance to anything, *how come you still feel that the world is at odds with you and something is sorely wrong?* You resonate deeply with the truth about how things are; yet your everyday life is a testimony to boredom, frustration, and discontent.

Here's the reason for these paradoxes: conditioning, by its nature, will continue to grab you over and over again. Patterns that have been running for decades seem to have a mind of their own. They continue to pull you in despite your best intentions not to identify with them. You desperately strive not to be triggered. Yet there you are, back in that old familiar, comfortable rut. You may have even experienced a profound glimpse of your true nature that lasted for months or even years—and still you find yourself playing out the same struggles that bring you unhappiness.

Dedication is the quality that will help you climb out of this low place. When you're dedicated, you're committed; you devote yourself and stay the course, even when it's hard. What are you dedicated to?

Nobody's asking you to change any patterns or behaviors. Peace doesn't require you to feel differently, clear your mind of troublesome thoughts, or kill the ego. Really, you don't need to eliminate or transform anything. I give you permission, right now, to officially give up trying to become a better person or improve your self-esteem.

Dedicate yourself to just one thing: being aware. What's real is that you're aware—and always have been. You're not the personal, separate entity that you may believe yourself to be. You are awareness itself, endlessly everywhere.

The pull to identify as a freestanding entity—with a body, mind, personality, and gender—is so seductive! But being dedicated invites you to realize, over and over, that awareness is what you really are. A painful feeling? Once you shift to being aware of it, you'll notice thoughts and physical sensations appearing. You don't need to change them—just welcome them as they are. An incessant monologue in your head? Shift to being aware, and you immediately become uninvolved with those thoughts.

Keep recognizing the truth of your experience with great precision, and ultimately you'll see that life is an unfolding flow of experience. There's no separate "you" in it. And in that realization, you'll find complete and utter peace.

You cannot enlighten yourself—because the separate self isn't real; the idea of it falls away. No one is here to do any enlightening. But you can stoke the fire of dedication by setting the stage for the thought-based structure of your personal self to collapse.

Stay dedicated to turning your attention inward toward your inner experience instead of staying lost in the world of objects. Remind yourself that repeating stories in your mind doesn't serve. Become an expert in how you suffer and realize what has changed in the moments when suffering ceases. Recognize where your thinking is constricted and play with bringing openness and flexibility to your mind. Feel the energy of separation, trying, and wanting in your body—and notice that your essential aliveness is never affected by any phenomena that arise in it.

> *"Feel the energy of separation, trying, and wanting in your body—and notice that your essential aliveness is never affected by any phenomena that arise in it."*

Rinse and repeat, as often as necessary, until doing falls away and the ease of being is revealed.

Stay focused on your search until focus is no longer needed. Investigate until there is no one left to do the investigating. Recognize the one thing that is real—which is not a thing at all.

It's simply being life as it births itself in the timeless now.

Compassion

As you become acquainted with automatic habits and how they have affected you, self-compassion is of great value. It's one of the ways that love manifests. And when you show compassion toward yourself, you'll find yourself acting kind, friendly, and tender toward everything that arises. You'll be aligned with the way things are, which is naturally accepting and compassionate.

If you are truly dedicated, you'll leave no stone unturned in the quest to let go of what's false and know what's true. When you welcome the defenses that allow you to suppress and avoid your experience, everything that's been hiding out in the shadows of your mind, heart, and body is seen in the light of effortless knowing. And this is where compassion is helpful.

Fear, shame, sorrow, resentments, beliefs, arrogance, compulsions—every single bit of it comes to be experienced. You open to these painful feelings and tell yourself the truth about your past misguided choices that came from fear and confusion. From the perspective of absolute reality, these experiences have never been judged or resisted. But you may very well find it difficult to welcome them without resisting. Compassion for yourself smooths the way.

What is compassion toward yourself? Let's break it down.

It's about being as kind to yourself as you would be with a child who is hurting. Instead of judging your thoughts or emotions, say, "Yes, this is here, I can let it be here." Treat yourself gently, rather than being dismissive or harsh; allow the difficult feelings and sensations in your body to just be.

Simply being aware is already compassionate. It's free of any content and doesn't avoid some experiences and prefer others. It's like air or space. It just is, without struggling or defending. Being aware is infinitely kind because you stop fighting your own experience. *Who you are is infinitely kind.*

If you've been rejecting your experience for a long time, compassion toward yourself might feel foreign at first. Like the rusty old Tin Man in *The Wizard of Oz*, you may creak and groan until you get used to it, especially if it's a large change for you. But here's the hidden gem in self-compassion: first, you have the courage to open fully to your experience. Then, you examine the line between you and what you're experiencing—and discover that it's not there! You're pure openness with no boundary. You've tapped into the unity of life where all is completely at peace with itself. This is you—here and everywhere!

Discover that beneath all the stress and struggle, your heart is naturally, boundlessly compassionate. It is your nature—how could it be otherwise?

Bring this compassion to the feelings you become aware of. And when you notice resistance—self-critical thinking, judging, defending, fear—you've rubbed against an identity created by conditioning: the one who judges, the guilty one, the one who doesn't want to be seen as less than perfect…

This is your moment to open fully with compassion. Let everything that's been hiding come out of the shadows.

Compassion offers the welcoming invitation to meet all the disowned and fragmented parts of yourself with the accepting heart of awareness. You no longer need to expend energy avoiding these experiences. Finally, you simply allow them to be, and you realize that who you are is the vast accepting space itself that is all-inclusive, undefended, and free.

Humility

Humility is at the heart of the investigation into true happiness. The biggest deterrent to discovering that you are already what you've been looking for is your sense of yourself as a separate person. The tentacles of this identity reach far and wide into everything you believe to be true. Humility helps you see through to the truth.

The functioning world consists mostly of beings who believe themselves to be separate, constantly bumping into one another. Each one has a strong sense of "I": "I know who I am, I know what I want, I know how I feel about myself, I have ideas about what I do and don't deserve, I know how things should be."

This is the nature of what we call life in the world, and it's far from peaceful or stress-free. Look at the surface of everyday life, and all you'll see is I, I, and more I. In fact, this belief in the separate self is at the core of both personal and global conflict, disharmony, and unease. It makes life feel complicated, and triggers the mental tendency to either hide in compulsive behaviors or think endlessly to try to figure it all out.

Being humble simplifies matters tremendously. When you're humble, you lose your sense of self-importance. Your sense of "I" (and everything attached to it) is no longer the center of your world. You let go of what you think you know and realize that you don't know. You give up what you think you need, and gracefully receive life's gifts. You relinquish the urge to control—to force things to be the way you think they should be—and surrender into what is.

As you dip your toe into the sea of humility, you cast away the anchors that keep things familiar and orderly. No longer relying on your assumptions and expectations, maybe you'll feel afraid of what might happen. Or maybe you'll be flooded with a great sense of relief because you can finally stop trying to control the uncontrollable.

Maintaining the sense of the personal "I," the limited, separate self, is actually an energy drain. It's a lot of work to sustain your stories, deal with your personal needs, and manage the feeling that there's something missing. You might not realize you're making this effort until you stop. This is why you feel so energized when you're caught up in the flow of an engaging activity. Our language says it perfectly: you lose yourself in the activity. Yes, you do! It's an incredible relief, and very relaxing, to lose the illusion of the personal self.

Humility invites you to empty yourself out. Pour out everything that makes you a separate person—your history, life experiences, desires, goals—even if you think there's nothing left. When you release all the objects that create your sense of you, you realize that you still exist. You're not located in any one place as a separate being, but you're here, unendingly alive and awake. You're empty of forms, and one with life itself.

The contraction into the separate self is painful and limiting. You must know this or you wouldn't be looking for a way out. But who is this one who is looking? Be open beyond any ideas you have about who you are or what absolute reality is like. Adopt an attitude of curiosity about everything you take for granted, and be infinitely receptive to all that appears. Dedicate yourself with diligence in the face of the power of conditioning, while softening into oceans of compassion. Be so humble that everything personal disappears.

And know that what you seek is always here now, endlessly peaceful, overflowing with possibility.

Explorations

Take each of these qualities, one by one. See if you can find them alive in you. Make space for them to flower. Feel the effect on your mind and body. If you notice resistance, investigate and welcome your experience. Keep it simple, and just do your best.

1. Openness—"I don't know anything. I am open to things exactly as they are."

2. Curiosity—Taking nothing for granted, ask, "What am I experiencing right now?" "What is it made of exactly?"

3. Receptivity—"I receive without avoiding, defending, or needing to control. And if I avoid, defend, or control, I receive that, too."

4. Dedication—"I stay dedicated to seeing through conditioning to discover peace and happiness."

5. Compassion—"I am infinitely kind to myself."

6. Humility—"I surrender my need to control, to have things be the way I want them to be."

Listen to the guided audio meditation at
www.GailBrenner.com/books.

4

Running and Staying

Now that you're grounded in being open, receptive, dedicated, and humble, we're going to explore the experience of emotions more directly. We tend to get so caught by our feelings, and we're terrified of getting to know them. So we'll start by looking at what an emotion actually is and why we get so stuck in them. Then we'll go deeper to learn how to unravel them.

It might sound like you've heard some of this before, but when it comes to emotions, you need to understand in depth how to approach them. What you'll find is that when you're fully present with your emotional experience, feelings stop making you feel separate and confused. See them clearly for what they are, and they'll lose their power to sidetrack you. Then you're here, as you are, enjoying life. Emotions will arise, but they will no longer touch the peace that you are.

My friend described his fear of his powerful emotions perfectly, "I'm a runner." He has struggled mightily with alcoholism, relationship troubles, anxiety, and living every day with a deep sense of dissatisfaction. Yet, he had that brilliant, self-reflective insight— the golden treasure: "I'm a runner." This crack in the facade of his mindless existence invites a slew of questions: How does it feel to run? What are you running from? What if you slowed down and took a look? What's so scary about stopping and being still?

Closing down to yourself is so painful. It pushes feelings aside, excluding them from conscious awareness. And that creates the impulse to run. Rather than staying and opening fully to your actual experience, you close down by eating, drinking, staying busy, gossiping, incessant texting, TV watching, endless thinking. Anything but the simple act of stopping and allowing yourself to meet and befriend what's here.

Avoiding the truth of the moment creates the identification of you as a separate self in a separate body. With your attention entangled in the mind, you believe that emotions are real. You're so distracted that you forget to notice that something else is here: the "being aware" that already welcomes everything.

The Pain of Closing

When you run from parts of yourself, you set up an inner war. Experiences appear—feelings, sensations in your body—yet you deny them. You turn away and pretend they don't exist or you react to them with anger and resistance. Meanwhile, you're preoccupied with your attention drawn into stories that make up your life circumstances, roles you play out, and behavior patterns that create the illusion of your limited identity. It's a kind of violence. You're fighting reality, evading the truth of the moment, cutting off a tender and valid experience that's part of the totality. And you mistakenly believe you're limited.

Yet, in our everyday world, this seems normal. As avoidance of feelings becomes a habit, our lives feel pressured and off-track. We have to keep moving because we're afraid to be quiet or alone. Society constantly bombards us with

> *"It's a kind of violence. You're fighting reality, evading the truth of the moment, cutting off a tender and valid experience that's part of the totality."*

messages that pull us away from ourselves—to buy more, do more, be more. And as soon as we're unhappy, we think we need pills or the next self-help fad to fix it. We're told that reality as we actually experience it is not okay. This is what we call life.

Every time you move away from the essence of your true nature, you avoid some aspect of your experience—and end up feeling fragmented. Part of you needs to stay hidden behind closed doors, while another part stands as sentry to make sure the secret feelings stay locked away. Meanwhile, you're out in the world—or stuck in your head—compulsively keeping yourself occupied so you don't feel the feelings. Life seems complex, disconnected, and confusing.

Things get even more complicated when these avoidance strategies turn into ways that you define yourself. You take on an identity: unworthy one, self-absorbed one, or one who is overwhelmed or depressed. You fall victim to these ways of being until you feel like you're imprisoned in a steel trap, and you're completely distracted from your essential core as aware presence. Yes, you're breathing, and the days pass. But who are you? Whose life is this? Were you meant to search and hope forever? You must be in there, somewhere.

The Root Cause of Habits

Take any problem you have—anything you do or any tendency you play out that doesn't serve you. If you unwind it back to its source, you'll find a feeling that you've been avoiding. And it's this unexamined feeling that makes you think you're separate. Say that you tend to be a people-pleaser. Shining a light on this tendency, you'll notice that sometimes you feel obligated to do what others want you to do. You might tell yourself a familiar story about what you have to do or what's expected of you. But if you look more directly at this feeling of obligation, you'll become aware of some inner discomfort, a sense of being ill at ease. And if you investigate even more closely, you might find feelings of fear, sadness, lack, or emptiness.

So there you are, out in the world, living through the lens of believing you need to please others. You might even feel resentful or depleted because of it. All your efforts are about trying to come to a place of peace within yourself, reasoning, "If I make them happy, they'll finally love and accept me." But with your attention outside yourself, grasping what you think you need, you're avoiding your innermost feelings. And you don't realize that the deepest peace is available, right here in any moment, by turning your kind and spacious attention *toward* understanding the nature of these feelings. Here is where you can discover that you're already whole, and here's where the possibility for seeing through this painful way of being resides.

Consider addictions, self-defeating behavior patterns, or interpersonal strife—avoidance of feelings is the culprit whenever you're suffering. Take a look at any area of your life that isn't working for you, and you'll surely find some challenging feelings lurking.

- Do you limit your expression in the world?
  Fear is driving you.

- Do you drink or eat too much?
  Some feeling is eating away at you or drowning you.

- Do you complain?
  You're likely to be irritated or disappointed.

- Are you emotionally triggered by certain people?
  Do you continually make self- defeating choices?
  You haven't yet discovered the feelings hidden outside your conscious awareness.

This is why you feel like a hamster on a wheel. When feelings are suppressed, they don't disappear. Instead, they run the show from behind the scenes. You're like a puppet, with unexplored emotions pulling your strings. These feelings push you to engage in behaviors and thought processes that falsely define you—and block the happiness you desire.

Avoiding Yourself, Reclaiming Your Self

And, oh, the effort it takes to manage unexplored feelings! You need to patrol your emotions so they don't overtake you, keep your defenses strong, stay intricately involved with the dramas in your life so there's no room to meet your feelings, and somehow deal with the resulting stress. Then, because you're unhappy, you get caught up in trying to change yourself for the better—by thinking more positively or pushing yourself to achieve or improve. It's like forming a perfect pile of sand on the beach and trying to maintain it exactly as is. It's exhausting and completely unsustainable.

Meanwhile, in the midst of all the turmoil, the essence of you as the fundamental fabric of life, luminous and present in every experience, is overlooked.

Dodging your emotions is saying "no" to life. You're given the full, glorious, inexpressible reality of the moment, but you choose what you think is acceptable and unacceptable. Then you live in fear that the parts you rejected will push through and overwhelm you. You become a traffic cop, letting some experiences pass through and limiting the flow of others. Distraction becomes a survival strategy to keep your most tender feelings at bay. "Limited self" becomes your name and identity.

When you avoid parts of your experience, you live a fear-based life, pieced together from what you allow in. It can never be satisfying, because it's built on a misconstrued idea of who you are. You long for peace and fulfillment that you think must be missing, yet you don't realize that all it takes is a simple shift of attention away from the objects of suffering and into the stable ground of pure being.

The journey back to wholeness, beyond the fragments and cut-off places within you, involves shining the light of presence on emotions that have been hiding out in the shadows. You realize pure presence—not to heal or fix anything, or to change your behavior, or become a better person—because the truth of you has never been broken. These are traps that reinforce the false belief about who you are—and miss the possibility of resting in presence, available right now.

Instead, you reclaim these forgotten realms of unexplored feeling because they're here, real, and valid. They're an aspect of pure reality that takes shape as feelings, a sacred manifestation of the whole of life to be honored, not shunned.

Why We Resist

Forgetting the totality of timeless, ever-present you and identifying as a separate, limited entity often begins in your reaction to events that occurred in childhood, which is reinforced over time if the reaction remains unexplored. As we've seen, any feeling that wasn't fully experienced goes underground, outside of conscious awareness, and gets lodged in the body and mind. From an early age, you are faced with a dilemma: how to go on and survive with the shadow of these emotions nipping at your heels and walling off your heart.

Some of us shut down and go numb, others endlessly try to figure out solutions. But all of us lose the experience of our true nature. We stray from our connection to beauty, tranquility, stillness, clarity, and ease. But all is not lost. It's the nature of life to offer blessed moments that serve as reminders—when you're deeply touched by love or beauty or overcome with pure glee, or wholly absorbed in the flow of experience. These tastes of being fully alive, which are completely problem-free, point to the possibility of weaving the apparent parts of you back together and realizing that who you are is way beyond their sum.

Exploring hidden emotions goes against the grain of everything we're taught. Who wants to feel the pain of boredom, terror, or rage? Certainly, your limited idea of yourself wants no part of it. But when you tap into your deepest questions and your desire to understand the absolute truth of things, you'll find that you're capable of experiencing everything. Your need to know the truth becomes more powerful than your need to resist and defend. When your willingness to be with things as they are trumps your fear of them, you've reached the turning point that opens up infinite potential.

We resist opening the doors to our inner world for a variety of reasons:

- Intense and painful feelings can be frightening or overwhelming.

- We feel out of control and don't know what to do with these feelings.

- We get temporary relief from certain behaviors or life circumstances.

- We have no role models to guide us.

- Our schools and families don't teach us how to be with feelings.

- Everything about our post modern, feel-good, stay-connected culture encourages us to deny the existence of our feelings.

Our focus on the jumble of our thoughts and on the world at large is reinforced, encouraged, and expected in our culture.

Keeping feelings veiled is the norm, the conventional way of being. And the result is a sense that something is fundamentally off or out-of-sync with us.

Trust that sense—because it's true.

With every good intention, you try to restore yourself. In fact, as convoluted as it seems, all your efforts have peace and happiness as their goal. If you drink to drown your feelings, you're trying to become peaceful. If you lash back in anger, it's about shutting someone down or pushing them away so you can purge yourself of your pain and return to peace. If you try to control or manipulate to get attention, you're seeking the satisfaction of being loved. If you fill your time with activities to escape from feeling bored, your goal is still happiness and respite from a perpetual sense of inadequacy.

You think you need to wage war to find peace—to slog through misery and self-criticism to finally deserve happiness.

Of course you want to be happy! But you look everywhere except in the right place—at the core of your present moment experience. You try to forget about what troubles you or pretend that everything is okay. You might play the "if only" game—if only I received an apology, if only the right partner showed up—postponing happiness to the imagined, idealized future. Maybe you wallow endlessly, and sometimes happily, in your emotions. Or maybe you're waiting for time to finally heal all wounds.

Some of these strategies may help for some time. But why not take the direct route to abiding peace?

Being with Everything

Rediscovering the full magnificence of who you are is radical, fierce, and loving. All of your hidden feelings are offered the space to be in the deepest acceptance.

"Rediscovering the full magnificence of who you are is radical, fierce, and loving."

You don't have to be concerned about changing anything about yourself. Simply welcome what is, as it is, fully. That's all. When you feel fear, it no longer drives you. When you meet shame and lack with clear seeing, you live from wholeness that has never been broken or damaged. By experiencing everything, the idea of you as separate falls away. Insights appear; new choices come to mind. You constantly emerge fresh and new, unhampered by the past. You're here! Awake, alive, unendingly resilient.

This is not a process of doing, but a flow of being. You don't have to learn special techniques or commit to any practices. You only need to accept the two-fold invitation: *stop and be aware.* Let the strategies you use to keep it all together unravel. Let yourself be uncomfortable as you discard your familiar coping methods. Allow the ground to be wobbly until you realize you can completely trust the fall into being—standing nowhere and everywhere at the same time.

Simply Stop and Be Aware

If the fire for happiness burns in you, there will be a moment of courage when you stop. Rather than playing out a habit once again—with the same unhappy result—you stop and let yourself be still. You step away from the force of conditioning that carries you. You feel the urge that appears, but you don't act on it, no matter how strongly you feel compelled to. This is it: the golden doorway to freedom.

Say that you compulsively overeat and dieting hasn't helped you. With the commitment to know the full truth, to see through all illusions to the actual reality of things, you take the radical approach, and you stop.

You stop putting the next morsel of food in your mouth. You stop buying into obsessive thoughts about planning your next meal or diet. You stop feeding the mental activity that rationalizes your behavior. You let yourself be still.

Stopping is the breath of fresh air that interrupts the momentum of old habits. It puts on the brakes so you can experience the feelings you'd been overlooking by unconsciously playing out the habit. You slow things down enough so you can see and feel the truth of your experience. You no longer let the habit propel you.

Stopping can be applied to any form of conditioning, any learned tendency that constricts you or makes you suffer. It's very simple. All you do is stop and take a look. Beginning with curiosity, you wonder, "What am I feeling when I snap back at my wife?" "What's going on inside when I want to run away after a conversation with my boss?" "What's behind my urge to shop or over-schedule or avoid family gatherings?"

When you stop, you see the truth of your actual experience—and it may be eye opening. You might become aware of fear that has been driving you, a sense of inadequacy that feeds the desire for approval, hidden shame or doubt or unworthiness, a body tied up in knots.

Once you realize what's been driving you, the possibility for freedom dawns. Before now, you'd been feeling out of control of your behavior, feeling like a victim of unseen forces within you. Despite your best intentions to help yourself, you knew you were still suffering. But how to get out of it remained a mystery.

Stopping the mindless, automatic behavior allows you to discover the feelings you'd been keeping out of conscious awareness. It marks the end of getting unconsciously carried away by emotions and the beginning of the return to yourself. To presence. To the truth of your experience.

As much as you can, bring space into your life. Be present and awake as you move through daily activities. Stop often and be aware of your experience. Begin to tell yourself the truth about what is actually happening within you. Practice spending a few moments in silence before going to sleep and just upon waking.

You're fertilizing the ground for some momentous discoveries.

The Anatomy of a Feeling

Feelings seem so real, and we make so much of them. Sadness, anger, fear, and irritation seem to be such an integral part of being human. Feelings draw our attention like a magnet, causing a lot of trouble in life. But when it comes to our quest for abiding peace and happiness, feelings deserve closer attention.

Let's take out the microscope and have a look. What exactly is a feeling?

First, you notice a label, say, "anxious." Naming an emotion helps you speak about your experience and communicate it with other people. It makes an experience known and concrete. When you say you feel anxious, we all think we know what you mean.

So if "anxious" is just a label for an experience, what is a feeling? What happens within you that makes you apply that label of anxious? Now you get to be aware of your inner experience, starting with what's happening in your body. What do you notice? You might sense tension in different areas, tightness in your chest or belly, shallow breathing, a band of contracted muscle across your forehead or in your jaw.

Are these anxiety itself, or simply physical sensations?

Then you might notice a stream of thinking: What's going to happen?…What if he doesn't call?…I have too many things to do…Why did I say that?… You become aware of a continually churning river of thoughts that flows without end, all with the themes of worry, fear, upset, and confusion. Are these thoughts anxiety?

When you examine the actual truth of anxiety, you find only physical sensations and thoughts—and a label that describes them. There's no actual thing called anxiety—or any other emotion.

Let's take another example: the bitterness and resentment you might feel over events that happened in your childhood. As you inquire, you'll find labels that describe those feelings— "bitter," "resentful," "hopeless," "sad." If you explore beneath the labels, you'll find a very familiar story you repeat in your mind about what happened, what should and shouldn't have happened, and what needs to happen now. And you may have been repeating this same story for decades.

But looking further, you'll discover physical sensations that have taken up residence in the body. You might find deep contractions, places that feel closed down, tightness that seems like you're wearing a suit of protective armor.

Over time, layers of sensation have piled up. Because they're unexplored, they fuel the repetitive story that keeps the past alive in you and drives unsatisfying patterns of behavior that seem out of control.

As you can see, a feeling is not an object. Although we talk about feelings and they seem real, when you investigate the truth of them, you see that they don't actually exist as separate things. What we call a feeling is actually a mix of physical sensations and a pattern of thoughts cycling through your mind.

The Blessed Journey Back to Your Self

When we take away this story-based thinking that brings unhappiness to your life, we see that these physical sensations have been present all along. What a discovery! At the heart of the turmoil in your life are these physical experiences of emotion.

Now let's go further and inquire more deeply into physical sensations. Do they have any inherent meaning? Are they real? They only have meaning if:

- They're ignored, which feeds the mind to keep stories alive, or

- They're consciously given meaning by the mind.
  (e.g., "A physical contraction *means that* I am anxious.")

But in and of themselves, with no words or meaning added, sensations are simply experiences that arise in awareness.

See for yourself. Close your eyes and ignore all thoughts, just for a moment. You'll notice the physical sensations. They might be intense or mild, pleasant or unpleasant, obvious or subtle. Now, shift your attention to being aware, and let the sensations be as they are. They might or might not change—your job is simply to be aware. If thoughts start to attract your attention, turn away from them and return to presence. What's here? Being aware—and sensations appearing in awareness.

Give yourself a hug! You've just done something absolutely revolutionary: You've inquired through to the core of your troubles and discovered that they stem from physical sensations with thoughts added in. Without the story (which we'll discuss in more detail in the next chapter), is there a problem? Can you allow physical sensations to be there and not avoid or label them? Of course you can. They aren't threatening or disturbing in their own right—unless you start thinking about them and attaching meaning. Experience only pure sensation—the experience arising in the moment—and there's no problem to be found.

We've established that what we call a feeling is the experience of thoughts and sensations. And we've seen that repeating the thought pattern overlooks the sensations and keeps the perception of a problem firmly in place. The more you go over the thoughts and try to find a solution to your perceived problems, the more you'll continue to feel stuck—because you haven't yet uncovered the real driver—unseen physical sensations.

> *"The more you go over the thoughts and try to find a solution to your perceived problems, the more you'll continue to feel stuck—because you haven't yet uncovered the real driver— unseen physical sensations."*

You also now know that physical sensations have no inherent meaning. And when you allow them to be experienced without changing them or interfering with their expression, they simply come and go, without any drama. And the real you—the being aware of them—is undisturbed. In the moment when there's no story grabbing your attention and physical sensations are experienced without avoiding them, suffering ceases. But don't take my word for it. See what your own direct experience reveals to you.

Realizing Pure Being

But there's another piece to this puzzle that makes the whole structure of your personal suffering collapse, and it's about discovering what's absolutely real. Anything temporary comes and goes; it isn't real—and sensations are temporary. They arise, change, and disappear.

So what's real? What's the deepest truth? Pure being cannot be described in words—because words are mental labels and true reality is just experience, free of all forms. At best, it's experienced as *This*. *This* is not a moment in time or a meeting of awareness and objects. *This* is the formless nature of life that appears in the timeless now. There's nothing personal in it—because there's no structure for the idea of a person to exist. It is existence itself without form or content. Pure being, with no one or no thing in it. It's empty and totally transparent.

Yet, here is the paradox: it includes everything. People, things, situations, time, stories, sensations are all part of the totality. It's impossible for anything to be separate from it, which is why all objects shine with the luminosity of pure presence. This is what everything is, at its essence.

Let's return to our experiment where you let the story go, your attention is on being aware, and you notice sensations occurring. If you let go of any idea that labels a sensation or defines a body that the sensation appears in, if all mind activity—including your identity as a separate entity—is turned off and experienced as just a ripple of energy without content, there is only *This*. You see that not even sensations are real. They have no power whatsoever. They, you, everything is one with the harmonious unfolding of life.

This, Being is limitless, timeless. It just is, and it is you. You have no boundary. You are the all, with nothing personal in it. You are everywhere, bursting with life and potential. Not in conflict, because there's nothing separate to be in conflict with. Not in resistance, because what is there to resist? It's all you!

In pure reality, there's no form—meaning no story, no feeling, no thought, no sensation, no you or other. In this understanding, being bothered by a problem or feeling simply isn't possible.

In the moment when all forms are seen and felt through, the house built on sand that you took to be you and your life falls apart completely. The experience of *This* is indescribable—but you might call it abiding happiness, more peaceful than anything you could imagine, a tender heart bursting with joy and celebration. You experience a physical ease, because all tensions and contractions are seen and released as they appear. Everything is ordinary, because there's the illusion of familiar forms—yet extraordinary in the awe of its very existence.

Yes, it's possible to live in this state. When the mind is needed, it functions. When responsibilities arise, they're taken care of thoroughly and efficiently. When planning makes sense for intelligent living, it happens. It's a blessed life, without suffering.

Rinse and Repeat

As we all know from our own experience, conditioned patterns are powerful. Forms congeal, forgetting happens, stories reconstruct themselves to seem so believable. Despite an unwavering commitment to know the truth, you wake up to realize you've been caught once again.

Don't take lightly the power of physical sensations to keep your feeling of separateness intact. We all have embedded patterns of physical reactions that are so established in the body that they easily stay outside of conscious awareness. And they may trigger painful memories and misperceptions of reality.

Every moment of welcoming physical sensations without a story or the label of a feeling is a moment of peace. Have no goal to feel better or remove feelings. Only offer the most loving space for these sensations to be felt with no resistance as often as the sensations appear.

Here's how suffering ends: these moments of consciously experiencing physical sensations short-circuit the story that defines you as a separate self. Let the sensations go unnoticed, and your story will run wild. Embrace them as they are, and you can see them as temporary appearances that have nothing to do with the truth of you. Then realize that as aware presence, there's no time for any ideas or sensations to surface. There's only *This*, pure being—which means that suffering isn't possible.

Practice this over and over, and your whole identity becomes unglued. Sensations are felt as they are without adding meaning.

Thoughts are mental noise. Loving presence simply is, at the heart of everything.

Your mantra is always "rinse and repeat." Every time you become aware that you're caught in an old habit, begin to unwind it and follow the breadcrumbs back to you: timeless, formless being.

- There's no such "thing" as a feeling.

- What you call a feeling consists of thoughts and physical sensations.

- Repeating thoughts as a story keeps the habit in place.

- Abandon thoughts, ideas, beliefs, and labels, so you can knowingly be that which is aware.

- Allow physical sensations to be, change, come, and go, without interfering.

- Recognize and experience the timeless quality of presence and see that not even a sensation is real.

- Realize that life simply is—still, silent, unified, undisturbed.

- This is you.

Have patience and keep the fire burning. Every time the structure of a habit collapses, it loses its fuel. And as you experience the effects of getting unstuck and the pleasures of freedom, your sensitivity grows. In the beginning, you may need to reflect several times during the day to discover when a habit took hold. Then, you'll become aware in the middle of playing it out. Eventually, you'll notice the urge as it starts to take shape. Each time is an opportunity to soften the force of the habit.

You're counteracting conditioning, seeing through your identity as a limited entity, and recognizing that everlasting peace is always available.

The Mind Will Try to Close You Down

In the quest to wake up from the trance of your illusory, separate self, the mind is a power to be reckoned with. If you listen to your mind, you'll undoubtedly stay stuck and unfulfilled.

The process of unwinding habitual ways of thinking and feeling, as laid out here, means the eventual death of any notion proclaiming that you're a separate entity. It means the end of being controlled by thoughts that appear in the mind. The thoughts don't necessarily disappear, but they're no longer taken as truth so they lose their grip on your attention.

> " *The process of unwinding habitual ways of thinking and feeling, as laid out here, means the end of being controlled by thoughts that appear in the mind.* "

The mind doesn't go easily when its power to control is threatened. You desire to know yourself as formless reality, yet the habitual power of thoughts stays firmly in place. You're fully committed to a laser-like exploration of the experiences that underlie mindless habits. Yet, the mind presents you with convincing thoughts that pull your attention away from yourself and into the world.

If any of these thoughts creeps in as you open fully to all of your experience, recognize that they have no essential meaning. They aren't valid or true, and they sustain suffering by involving your attention in automatic habits, reactions, and sensations.

- I'm too weak to explore emotional pain.

- It's not possible for me to be happy.

- I'm afraid I'll be overwhelmed and won't be able to handle it.

- If I feel the pain, I might cry forever.

- I prefer familiar discomfort to the unknown.

- I feel justified in staying stuck because I was wronged.

- It's someone else's responsibility to make this better for me.

- If I let go, I'm approving others' bad behavior.

- I need an apology.

If you believe any of these thoughts, your identity as a victim will remain and you'll wonder why you can't figure out how to be happy. In truth, they're mental energy with words attached that have no essential meaning—unless you give them meaning through the power of your belief. These thoughts are a false proxy for who you already are. Instead, discover that even when these thoughts appear, you're aware. Live here. Explore the nature of awareness beyond emotions and mental ideas.

You will find yourself, utterly intimate with all.

Explorations

1. Be honest with yourself about how you resist your experience. What do you do that keeps your attention occupied elsewhere? What propels you to stay in your head and avoid your emotions? What drives you? Consider that these are conditioned patterns and not who you really are.

   All this activity arises in the truth of you. You can return home in any moment with a shift of attention.

2. A few times a day, or more, stop and be aware. What do you stop? Doing, planning, analyzing, worrying, making things happen. Simply stop and take a breath. Then be aware of your in-the-moment experience. Just notice what's present.

3. What's a feeling? Recognize that a feeling always has a physical component. As often as you remember, stop, be aware, and establish yourself as a welcoming presence to physical sensations.

4. It's possible to be aware without being aware *of* anything. See if you can let your attention rest as awareness. Objects may seem to come and go, but stay as awareness. Let go of doing to realize being.

It's okay if you get scared. Your mind isn't used to this experience of complete peace.

Listen to the guided audio meditation at www.GailBrenner.com/books.

5

The Puzzle of Thinking

We're beginning to understand how powerful thoughts are to capture your attention and mislead you into believing false ideas about yourself and the world. If you experience that vague feeling that something isn't right, take a look at the thoughts running through your mind. You're bound to discover judgments, worries, and regrets.

But what about the useful functions of the mind? Where would you be without labeling, planning, and understanding how things work? Thoughts turn formless reality into familiar forms and create language that allows us to communicate with each other. With the mind, we make sense of the world. We know what things are, and what to expect. We feel in control.

Thoughts that you're not attached to are not problematic. These are random, neutral thoughts, or the ones that express creative ideas and help you live in the world. You need to know something, and a thought appears bearing an answer or solution. A unique idea arises, and joyful creation results. These thoughts aren't sticky, repetitive, or laden with emotion.

But attachment to thoughts is a different story. These are the thoughts that don't just float by; they stick. You might spend your precious time pondering your unfulfilling life circumstances or replaying internal monologues about what you should or shouldn't have said. You endlessly analyze situations that may have ended years ago or recycle "what-if" scenarios. Or, you're frustrated when the expectations you hold about what should happen don't pan out.

The mind gets absorbed in the obsessive and mundane—while you overlook the contentment and ease that are your natural state.

When we take the content of thoughts to be true, they create the illusion that things are not okay as they are. They judge, evaluate, and separate, giving the impression that something is wrong or lacking. When thinking reigns supreme, you will feel ill at ease and unhappy. How could it be any other way?

> *" When we take the content of thoughts to be true, they create the illusion that things are not okay as they are."*

Thoughts tell us not to accept things as they are. They resist by giving a resounding "No!" to the natural flow of life, saying:

- "No, not this."

- "It should be different."

- "I don't want it to be this way."

Reality is always effortlessly unfolding, no matter what thoughts appear. Even a split second of letting go of thinking will show you how peaceful it is to simply receive things as they are. Add in the mind's nitpicking commentary, and a problem will appear before you know it. But remember this: thoughts are not your absolute reality. Even though thoughts are troubled, they arise in the lovely, open space of you. The ocean's surface may be agitated by a storm, yet the depths remain still and unmoving.

If you live by following the apparent "reality" of thoughts, your life will be stormy. But know yourself as aware presence, and you are peaceful and serene, no matter what appears.

No Need to Stop Thoughts

It's a common misconception to believe that you need to stop the mind so that you can be peaceful and happy. Well, you're off the hook, because stopping thoughts isn't necessary.

Trying to stop the mind creates effort and agitation and puts you at war with yourself. If a thought arises naturally, and you tell yourself that you need to eliminate it, all you've done is create resistance by thinking more. And if you're trying to stop the mind, who is doing the trying? This is an endeavor of the personal self that makes you think you need to expend effort to be different than you are—a great misunderstanding.

But here's the secret that investigating thought reveals. You will find, as you meticulously inquire into the nature of thinking, that thoughts arise then disappear, along with the illusion of the one who thinks them. "You" aren't stopping thoughts. They are known to be insubstantial, temporary appearances that have no independent meaning or power. And the natural quiet of an awakened mind is revealed.

Nothing at all needs to change for you to realize that you're infinite, aware presence. Not one single thought needs to disappear or transform. You simply correct this case of mistaken identity by recognizing that you're not defined by the content of your thoughts. Instead, you are the awareness that thinking arises in. Before any thoughts—and in the midst of the most severe cyclone of thoughts—you're simply aware. And knowing the timeless nature of reality, what we call a thought doesn't even have time to take shape.

We can play in the world of thought, but at the same time know that it's not the true reality.

A thought by itself is not a problem. It's simply a wisp of energy arising in awareness. But when the content of a thought is personal to you, the separate self, and especially if it is charged by suppressed emotion, it temporarily defines your reality. These are compulsive thoughts about how to make sense of things, cope, and restore the peace you think you're missing. Buying into these thoughts reduces the all-encompassing vastness of you to the mere fraction of itself that you believe it is. And while you're busy thinking, you're missing the fact of you—here, alive, aware, and at peace.

The medicine for the dilemma of thinking isn't to banish thoughts. And it isn't to indulge in them in an effort to solve endless problems. It's much simpler: you make peace with thinking by understanding and losing interest in it. *You don't try to stop thoughts; you stop listening to them.* A thought appears, and you don't pay attention to it—so it doesn't disturb you. It's seen as meaningless and irrelevant. And as your interest in thinking subsides, you recognize that most of it is not only unnecessary, but stressful and agitating as well.

First, you understand that you don't need to make yourself think in order to function. You start trusting the natural intelligence of life that's always been here. And when you're out of the way, you see that it offers exactly what you need, with only practical thinking required. Then, you realize that you *are* life—with no thoughts and no one who thinks them. Your exquisite, transparent self shines everywhere.

The thinking mind is a force to be reckoned with. It consumes your attention and defines your everyday reality. Lose interest in it? That might sound unfathomable to you.

And that's where this chapter will help. Acquaint yourself with how the mind works, so you can recognize when thinking is in control. Feel the impact of the mind-driven life that most of us live, and dip your toe into another possibility—that you don't need to let your thoughts rule, that life is just fine without most of your thoughts. Then question the limited, scared one who believes she needs to think to function. And step through the doorway of boundless peace and uncontainable joy.

Why We Think

As humans, we love to know, and we get anxious when we don't know. Our physical bodies are designed for survival, and we're wired to be highly alert to threats. Things that are mysterious, unknown, or out of control frighten us.

Our developed brains make us capable of thinking—and this capacity helps us to cope with threats and our fear of the unknown. Thinking helps us navigate life; it tells us which way to go and what to expect when we get there. It attempts to quell the fears so we feel secure.

When thinking goes overboard, we get caught in complicated belief systems that try to predict and control reality. We develop clear ideas about how things should be, what we want to have happen, and what's acceptable. And we apply these ideas constantly in our day-to-day living.

Can you imagine waking up in the morning and having no idea how your day will play out? This is the actual nature of life—your life. No matter what you plan, expect, or hope for, life evolves as it does. Things happen as they happen. Yes, it's enjoyable and relaxing when life matches your expectations— but what if it doesn't? What if you lose the deal...get laid off... your wife tells you she's leaving you?

Living according to your beliefs and assumptions is like trying to move around a small room packed with furniture. Everywhere you turn, you bump into something. It's far from smooth sailing because you constantly encounter frustration and disappointment.

Being stuck in thought creates a false representation of reality. There's a saying, "The map is not the territory." You can study a trail map all day, but you won't know the territory until you begin walking. Likewise, believing expectations about how things should be will always mask your direct experience of reality. Let them go, and you're here, ready to open up to the true nature of existence. You stop resisting what's here. You say "Yes!" to life as it's offered.

Life simply is—present, silent, untroubled, undisturbed, at peace. It has no interest in the past or future. When you're afraid of losing control, when you're laboring under the burdens of the past, or when you fear the vastness of you—the mind kicks into gear. It has mantras like, "Keep things manageable and safe" and, "Don't go outside your comfort zone." Then, when life conflicts with your needs—when what it brings you is risky, uncomfortable, or unexpected—fear triggers the mind to spin out of control. You become consumed by obsessive, incessant thinking filled with what-ifs and if-only's. It's a life lived on edge, ruled by fear, and remote from aware presence. Does this sound familiar?

Good news: you can always find your way home. You can learn to recognize fear and fear-infused thoughts so they don't need to hide outside of awareness. You can explore beyond your known experience to reconnect with the freshness of presence. You'll probably feel lighter and less stressed—but don't stop there! Inquire into the nature of thoughts and thinking. Can thinking exist without awareness? Who thinks? Who is aware?

> *"Experience reality prior to language or any other thought. Here you are, as you've always been… luminous, alive, and awake."*

Let your attachment to all thoughts fall away. Thoughts can arise, but you pay them no mind. Experience reality prior to language or any other thought. Here you are, as you've always been…luminous, alive, and awake.

So Many Thoughts

You're probably aware of the constant running commentary of thoughts going on in your mind. Left unexplored, they create unease and dissatisfaction. They bombard you with messages that you and the situations you're in are not okay. They say "no" to the present and keep you enslaved to the hope for a better future.

Whether these thoughts flood in like a tsunami or steadily gnaw on you—or both, it will serve you well to learn to recognize them. The act of recognizing a thought, rather than mindlessly being consumed by it, is a great step toward freedom. Your relationship to the thought changes completely. *When you observe a thought, you're no longer feeding it—and you begin to see it as mental noise, rather than a statement of truth.*

Let's take a simple thought such as, "I shouldn't have said that to her." If it appears without being noticed, it can breed all kinds of trouble, such as spinning in negative thinking about yourself, feelings of frustration and regret, and a general identity as someone who isn't good enough. Some people get stuck in a thought like this for days.

But what is this thought, really? It's a temporary appearance made of words and sounds, and it is *not* a description of what is real or meaningful. See it this way, as it really is, and it's power to grab you dissolves. Allow the habit of thinking to subside by not getting absorbed into the content of thoughts. I know, this is a revolutionary perspective, but it's true—and it's the key to happiness.

You can recognize thoughts by their ability to divide and separate. Here are three examples:

1. Thoughts that contain a "should" or "shouldn't" place a condition on infinite consciousness. Consider these:

   - Bad things shouldn't happen to good people.

- Marriages should last forever.

- I should make a killing in the stock market.

- My son should go to college.

Looking with the eyes of truth, these beliefs and expectations are nonsense; they don't reflect reality. Things either happen or they don't, and thoughts like these have nothing to do with it. But when you stick to them as your guiding principles in life, you're bound to be disappointed. How do you react when these expectations aren't met?

2. The inner judging voice, sometimes called the inner critic, is harsh and negative. It assumes the worst about you and devalues others. Believing this voice makes you feel lacking, alienated, hopeless, and alone. And it painfully limits your expression in the world.

3. Doubting and worrying show mistrust in the natural order of things—second-guessing everything. If you find yourself incessantly asking questions about what will happen or what should have happened, your mind paralyzes you. Unrecognized worrying expresses a terror of the unknown—which makes for a stressful and agitated existence.

These thought patterns are limiting and divisive and you easily take them on as your identity. Do you recognize yourself in any of them? As much as you think they define you, remember that they're a mistaken identity, a house built on sand. What is present when thoughts appear? Awareness—that which just is, free of time, free of form, infinitely peaceful. Thoughts aren't separate from awareness. They are forms that arise for a time then disappear back to formless being. They may grab your attention and create a belief about who you think you are. But the truth is always shining through. Rest in awareness, and thoughts don't even exist. See them as neutral arisings that have nothing to do with reality, nothing to do with the essential magnificence of you.

The Stories We Tell Ourselves

Just as toddlers like to hear the same books read over and over, we get enthralled by the stories that we tell ourselves. Repeatedly, we spin tales about not being good enough...or how the past shouldn't have happened the way it did...or why people should behave differently. We hold grudges and long for revenge. We gossip about the dramas in our everyday lives. We weave endless narratives about who we are and who we aren't and what we hope to be in the better, imagined future.

Storytelling views the world through the lens of the mind. It divides the totality of experience into good and bad, right and wrong, you and other—keeping you stuck in a falsely narrow perspective. If you look at a familiar story, you'll see that it's filled with mind activity. It beckons you to endlessly analyze, interpret, compare, and evaluate. The misidentified separate self takes these tales seriously and could chew on them forever.

When you focus on your internal storytelling, the stories become real to you, and you set yourself up for unhappiness, turmoil, and confusion. How to discover lasting happiness? Become aware of the stories you tell yourself, then simply let them be. Even if you believe they describe you and your circumstances, experiment with a different identity just for a moment—one that's unlimited, infinitely accepting, and utterly compassionate. Feel this possibility in every cell of your being.

Freedom from the Power of Thinking

Until you know differently, thinking makes you feel like you exist as a separate person. For your whole life, this strongly reinforced habit has been at the core of your personal suffering.

If your attention shifts from thoughts to being aware, the truth immediately becomes apparent: thoughts aren't real or true. How to unglue your attention from thinking? With precise and direct investigation.

Here are some ways to loosen the bond between thinking and attention so you're more available to life. These are breadcrumbs to pick up as you find your way home. They'll help you discern the real from the unreal and show you the joys of thought-free reality.

Inquire

Inquiry is a beautiful process that invites you into your present moment experience. You let go of the mind's overwhelming need to know, and pose a genuine question from a place of curiosity. As you inquire, let yourself not know the answer, then listen deeply to what arises.

Inquiry is a healing balm for an out-of-control mind. Rather than continuing on a thought-filled trajectory, you put the brakes on forward moving energy, stop, and ask questions. Who knows what you will discover? Simply be open to receiving what appears.

There are two ways to inquire into thoughts. First, you question the content of thoughts and the role of thinking. Then, you investigate the nature of thought and follow it back to its source—You!

When you notice that you're gripped by thoughts, ask these questions:

- What is this thing called a thought? Is it absolutely true?

- Do I need this thought? Is it essential?

- Does it serve me or anyone else? Is it helpful or useful?

- Is this thought agitating—or relaxing?

- Am I attached to it? Can I let it go?

You may be surprised to discover how many thoughts are repetitive and useless. They appear by habit, but with investigation, you see that they're damaging, painful, and at least unnecessary. This may be enough to let go of your connection to them.

Once you become aware of the futility of most of your thinking, the natural, sane choice that arises is to let it be—then you're effortlessly aware. Inquiry isn't about getting rid of thoughts. That happens by itself once you realize that they're conditioned fantasies that sabotage your happiness.

As redundant, worrisome thinking ceases to grab you, you're likely to feel lighter and brighter. You'll notice more space—gaps between thoughts. Enjoy the peace that comes, then go further to inquire, "What is a thought? Who is the one thinking?"

Take any thought, for example, "I'm going out for a walk." It takes time for each word to arise and the meaning of the thought to be understood. From the perspective of pure, timeless being, a thought has no time to form, so it can't actually exist. That's right! Any thoughts that appear seem real, but, take away the time needed for them to form, and they collapse.

Let this understanding seep into even your sticky and compulsive thoughts. When they arise, you have the opportunity to inquire into their nature, and you'll find your way home.

And who is the one thinking? Realize that you, as the separate self, don't create your thoughts. In fact, if you don't think of yourself as separate and limited, who are you? Question the idea of separation, and you'll know yourself as fully here, palpably alive, the life force at the core of everything. This can be trusted.

Lose Interest

Losing interest in thoughts may sound like an impossible task—but you—as awareness, as your true nature—already know how to have no interest in them. Many thoughts pass through your mind in the course of the day without troubling you. They don't stick, and they leave no residue. Why? Because you aren't interested in them. They come…they go—no problem.

But when thoughts are fueled by emotion, you're drawn to pay attention to them. You think them over and over and embellish them by telling yourself sad and scary stories. The mere appearance of thoughts isn't a problem—but feeding them with attention gives them a life of their own. They easily grow out of control, leaving you defined by them, anxious and unhappy.

But what if thoughts could appear without your being hooked by them? You disengage from the content of the thought itself by centering your attention in pure being. The thought can't help but lose its meaning and importance, and it can't define who you are.

The habitual nature of thinking may make it difficult to rest as awareness. You may have been thinking certain patterns of thoughts in exactly the same way for decades. They're highly conditioned, so much so that they have become your reality. To begin, it takes effort to disengage with thinking and with your identity as a thinking person—to discover the truth of you that's fresh and alive. As you take a stand in the peace your heart really wants, as you say no to what doesn't serve—as many times as necessary—thinking loses its importance.

> "As you take a stand in the peace your heart really wants, as you say no to what doesn't serve as many times as necessary thinking loses its importance."

You're letting a thought be what it actually is—nothing. It floats on by, dissolves, or disappears, and you remain. You're not pulled into the past or present, but here, peaceful, beautifully open and available to life as it actually is—not as how you think it should be.

A friend has a concise, powerful, long-standing thought: "Nervous breakdown." Given her family history, she's feared a nervous breakdown for a long time, and this phrase has become like a mantra to her. The effects? Terror, sadness, anticipating the dreaded event—reactions guaranteed to erode her happiness. But what if she could see this thought as nothing? It appears, but she gives it no consideration, and she remains here, untouched by it.

Make a practice of neutralizing your attachment to thinking as much as possible during your daily life. Try these, and any other creative ideas you come up with:

- Turn away from thoughts
- Throw them in the imaginary trash
- Just say "no" to them
- Drop them
- Let them go
- Put them down
- Remind yourself that the thoughts aren't helping you
- See that they're just sound in your head
- Experience them like they are speaking in a language you don't understand
- Hear them say gibberish, "Blah, blah, blah…"
- A suggestion from a friend: "Tune them out like my kids tune out my nagging."

In the spirit of truth and authenticity, lose interest in your thinking—because thoughts aren't real and their content isn't true. Without being driven by thoughts, your made-up, constructed life falls away, and you see you're not just present, but alive and overflowing with potential and joy.

Feel the Impact of Thinking

One beautiful afternoon, I was lying on a chaise lounge, relaxed and quiet, enjoying the warmth of the sun. A thought appeared, and immediately I noticed tension and contraction in my body. I let the thought go, and the contraction subsided. I switched back and forth a few times between thought and no-thought. What a discovery! I perceived the direct connection between the effort of thinking and the physical contraction it created—and the release of the contraction when I shifted my focus away from the thought and returned to presence.

Explore in your own experience, and you'll find that all sticky thoughts—the agitated and emotional ones that won't let go—are accompanied by anxiety, tension, and contraction. When you tell yourself the truth about how these thoughts impact you, the intelligent choice is to rediscover yourself as aware and alive.

With fresh eyes, you see clearly that being carried away by beliefs confines your brilliance. Storytelling entangles your body and mind. *These are old, repetitive thought patterns that have nothing to do with what's real in this now moment.* As you consciously experience the effects of thinking, you feel the pain of judging, worrying, and ruminating. And you gain insight into what makes you suffer—and how you can be free.

Recognize the impact of the thought-driven life, and you'll naturally begin to orient toward wholeness and ease.

This investigation of thinking isn't an exercise in self-blame; that would just be more agitated thought. There's nothing wrong with thinking. The thought patterns that plague you are understandable. You learned these strategies over the course of your life to help you manage in the world and avoid painful feelings.

But once your interest in truth is ignited, you're on fire to see things as they actually are. Then, knowing the end of suffering is possible, you can finally open to an honest exploration of how your thoughts have made you feel separate from your true nature.

Let thoughts be, without eliminating or indulging them. From the space of awareness that's completely accepting and never in conflict with anything, notice the effects of these tendencies of thinking. When you spin in doubt, criticize others, or repeatedly narrate a story of inadequate you, how do you feel? Are you stressed or relaxed, anxious or peaceful? What's the effect on your life circumstances and on the people around you?

Take time with this inquiry. Let it live in you as long as is necessary until thinking no longer disrupts you. Have patience with highly conditioned thinking patterns. They will return many times. But each time is an opportunity to recognize the truth of you.

Feel Feelings That Fuel Thoughts

You may have already discovered that emotions are often connected to compulsive thinking. Not only are thoughts flooding your mind, but you feel something as well—fear, anxiety, anger, sorrow. If these feelings aren't fully seen, they could be driving the force of your thinking.

When you can't stop thinking about a situation you wish had been different, your thoughts are filled with "shoulds" and "if-only's." If you peel the layers of the onion to see your experience underneath the thoughts, what do you notice? Self-judgment? Fear? Neediness? The despair of separation? A sense that you lack what you think you need to be worthwhile and whole?

Take any habit of thinking, and you'll find that feelings underlie it: Fears about what the future might bring and how you will react...anger at yourself for failing or at others for failing you...disappointment...rage...sadness...the list is endless.

Remember that as humans, we're built for survival. Unexplored emotions give us the sense that something's wrong. And the mind interprets that as a threat. The mind then tries to fix it—to make everything okay and safe once again. That's the beginning of a compulsive thinking pattern.

You can cut through this process by shining the light fully on your direct experience of the emotions that fuel thinking. Welcoming the feelings means that the mind no longer needs to think compulsively to figure it all out. Rather than using complicated mental strategies to avoid difficult feelings, you're simply here as aware presence, being with whatever arises. The structure of the divided, limited self collapses as you return to your natural wholeness. The pull to persistently think subsides.

Remember that a feeling is composed of bodily sensations with a compelling story attached. When you're caught in a whirlwind of thinking, look deeper to be present with all of your direct experience. If you truly turn away from thoughts—which we already know are nothing—you'll discover sensations in your body. Open fully to these sensations, welcome them, allow them to be. Feel whatever you feel—heaviness, tingling, burning, vibration. The space of awareness in which the sensations arise can encompass all of those. You're infinitely accepting of all, just as it is.

You may notice in the moments of allowing the sensations that thinking tapers off or doesn't grab you like it did. This is a wonderful discovery! When you take away the fuel of unexplored feelings, the need for excessive mental activity diminishes. Thoughts may continue due to the momentum of habit, but they become like clouds passing across the open sky of you.

Expand Attention Beyond Thinking Habits

Obsessive patterns of thinking keep you locked in to a very limited point of view. In an endless loop, you repeat thoughts about yourself, others, and circumstances in the world, day after day, year after year. A groove gets etched in your brain, giving you tunnel vision that sees things only one way.

Most often, thoughts like these have a negative tone. For instance, if you feel unresolved about a past situation, you'll rehash the story about what happened, replaying thoughts about what everyone should and shouldn't have done and how you were wronged. Although you might feel justified, the net effect is that you fall more deeply into the hole of suffering.

Some people are caught in anxious thoughts about the future. You worry about what will happen and expect the worst. You might compulsively plan in an effort to ward off the inevitable unknown. And you move through life feeling anxious and ill at ease, waking up in the mornings with a dark cloud already encircling your head before you even get going.

These thinking habits are restrictive. They take the whole of reality—with its infinite potential—then randomly pick out a tiny piece and call it true. It's like imprisoning a fish in a very small cage when the entire ocean is available. Wonder, flexibility, and heart go missing.

Once you recognize this constricting habit, expand your view. Take away the veil of familiarity, and try on the possibility of knowing nothing. Be so open that anything can happen. Then you're available to what's actually here. You're now aligned with the unfolding of life.

When you let the filters of thought fall away, you may make some important discoveries. Your expectations and one-way thinking have kept you unknowingly bound up, identified as a separate person—anxious and disheartened, trying to find solutions. When you expand out of your limited view to experience all that's real, you're knowingly conscious and alive. From here, you're free of mental habits and aligned with the infinite possibility that anything could emerge. You receive rather than control. Fresh and creative ways to address situations may come to mind effortlessly. You seem to gain clarity—but really, it was always available, just obscured by repetitive thinking.

As you step away from a thought pattern that's been playing for years, you may be in unfamiliar territory. As all the thought structures dissolve, you may be so open that it feels like your brain is rearranging itself. Let this openness pervade all of you. Then realize that this openness *is* you. Without being trapped by familiar thought patterns, you're present, awake, and alert. You're filled with potential, but unconcerned about what will happen next. You're pure receptivity.

Identification with thoughts is at the source of suffering and unhappiness. Inquire into these thoughts to determine if they're useful. Stop feeding them, and realize that without relying on them, you're still here as presence itself. Feel into the suffering that thoughts produce, and lose the tunnel vision that repetitive patterns create. Return again and again to knowing yourself as silent awareness.

> " *Feel into the suffering that thoughts produce, and lose the tunnel vision that repetitive patterns create. Return again and again to knowing yourself as silent awareness.* "

When you no longer need these techniques, they'll disappear. But use them wholeheartedly if they help. When your mind captures your attention, effortlessly return to the aware presence of you—empty of constricting thought forms, but overflowing with beauty, joy, tenderness, and love.

The End of the Mind-Driven Life

If you want to live in ever-present happiness, consider the end of the mind-driven life. Take everything you know, everything that defines you, and throw it into the holy fire. Surrender any thoughts you're holding on to—any ideas, attachments, hopes, desires, preferences. Open every cell of your being. Listen deeply, with nothing in the way—no expectations at all about what you'll discover. Be so devoid of any personal will that you're open to embracing whatever appears.

Then, go forth and enjoy yourself. Here's what you might discover:

- No more resistance to anything that happens. (It takes a belief or expectation to resist.)

- No more unwanted stress. (Stress is based on shoulds, have-tos, and musts—all thoughts.)

- No more person who thinks he must be in control. (You recognize the personal, separate self as simply thoughts, preferences, and feelings. There's no real entity that is you.)

- Clarity. (Without the confusion of thoughts, fresh insights appear. What to do becomes obvious.)

- Well being. (Quiet mind, calm, happiness)

- Love and compassion. (With the ending of absorption in personal dramas, true love is unleashed.)

- Endless peace.

But don't strive for these results—because who is it who is striving? The limited identity that causes the trouble in the first place. There's nothing to attain and nowhere to get to. In this very moment, you already are your natural self. Let all false structures go. And here you are—present, awake, and aware.

Explorations

1. Sit quietly and watch your experience. Notice the difference between thinking and attachment to thinking. Thoughts can appear that cause great disturbance, and thoughts can appear that cause no ripple whatsoever. There's no need to get rid of thoughts or squelch thinking. When your attention rests as awareness, with no attachment to thoughts, you see that thoughts simply arise in the totality of You.

2. When you're caught in a reaction to something or someone, stop and explore your experience. What beliefs are present? Are they true and real? What emotions are fueling the thoughts? Now, untangle awareness from these thoughts and feelings. Notice you have the option to simply be aware as objects float by.

3. What stories do you tell yourself about yourself? What do you believe to be your identity? If your true identity isn't defined by these thoughts, who are you?

4. Deep inquiry into thought (from page 98):
   - Do I need this thought? Is it essential?
   - Does it serve me or anyone else?
     Is it helpful or useful?
   - Is this thought agitating—or relaxing?
   - Am I attached to it? Can I let it go?

5. If you are in a tsunami of thinking, bring your attention out of your head and into your body. Be aware, loving presence in which the physical sensations appear.

   Listen to the guided audio meditation at
   www.GailBrenner.com/books.

6

Kidnapped by Fear

By now you know that the belief that you're a separate person—with gender, age, ethnicity, roles, and personality characteristics—is at the root of your suffering. This highly conditioned belief is reinforced by everyone: parents, schools, advertising, work, social groups, culture, and society in general.

How wonderful to learn that there's a solution to this problem of suffering! You abandon thought as the foundation of your reality and see through to the truth of emotions. You realize that you're so alive, you can't ever be contained.

This realization isn't conceptual—it's the palpable truth that becomes obvious in the moments of your life. But if you see signs that something isn't working, you need to inquire more deeply. Maybe you wake up in the mornings with a sense of anxiety or dread, or feel you're missing something you need to be happy. Maybe your interactions with others are frustrating, or you feel generally unsatisfied and disconnected. Maybe you've been depressed for a long time.

At the Heart of Suffering: Fear and Lack

All problems are driven by fear, a sense of inadequacy, or both. Fear is a largely physical response that gets the mind spinning with meaningless projections into the imagined, negative future.

It's about making up scary stories, then believing them. And the belief in inadequacy—a prominent disease in these modern times—has become firmly entrenched in our individual and collective psyches. Both subtly keep you hooked on suffering—and on the effort you expend to relieve that suffering.

> "*All problems are driven by fear, a sense of inadequacy, or both.*"

When you hold onto an identity that makes you feel separate, you live with a sense that things are not okay. You believe that you're incomplete and not enough. You're afraid to live and afraid to die. You can't simply be present—because this false identity keeps you wary of the unexpected and the unknown. You busily attempt to manage, control, and oversee as if your life depended on it.

You try desperately to find happiness somewhere out there, which breeds the longing of "if only." If only I could figure out my problems…if only the right partner or job would come along…if only things had been different…if only things would happen the way I want them to. The separate self can never be fulfilled. So all the things you want—peace, ease, well being—are delayed…and delayed…and delayed until a better future comes along.

It's an unending cycle of dissatisfaction. That better future never comes because it exists only as a thought in your mind.

In truth, it's always only now. Waiting for an improvement in your life circumstances keeps you from noticing that you're right here, already at peace. Preoccupied by hope for the future, you ignore the fact that you're caught in habits of fear and lack. And you're distracted from directly examining the disturbance that makes you suffer. The possibility of recognizing still, silent presence is all but forgotten.

As you recognize the futility of looking outward for happiness, fresh possibilities open up. What are you taking for granted that isn't true? What underlies the identification as the separate self, and how can you dispel it? What are you beyond the conditioned habits that seem so real?

Getting to the Root of the Problem

Living according to fear and lack keeps you right in your comfort zone, which, if you're honest, isn't that comfortable. You cling to familiarity, finding some relief in thinking you know who you are, what will happen, and how you'll respond. The known feels safe, while the unknown seems disconcerting, mysterious, and uncertain. We're so averse to the unknown that we often choose the familiar but unpleasant consequences of painful habits, instead of risking something new, fresh, and unfamiliar.

Anyone in any close relationship has experienced this phenomenon. You could recite from memory the script you and your partner or parent or child repeat whenever you're triggered. And you act out this script over and over, sometimes for years. You repeatedly choose to stay locked in this unsatisfying dance, with pride or fear blocking you from accessing innumerable other ways of being. At the risk of sounding unprofessional, I'd call it crazy. Wouldn't you?

Change happens easily, once you're willing to step out of your comfort zone and forget *everything* you already know. You meet the seeds of fear and lack with a boundless heart, and your constricted view expands to include infinite possibilities. You're released from this self-imposed prison and able to live as the natural intelligence of life. But this level of complete openness, where you're willing to embrace whatever arises, is rare.

Waking up to the truth of who you are invites you to *be* rare—to investigate to the core of identity. Once you become aware of the subtle ways the separate self is constructed, you find space for its dissolution. Identity thrives on ignorance, avoidance, and lack of clarity. It dissolves in the face of truthful investigation and clear seeing.

Shine the light of presence on the roots of identity: what appears are fear and inadequacy. Let presence liberate the secret beliefs and subtle sensations that keep you convincing yourself that you're separate. Let everything you know burn to ash as you realize that you've always been free.

The Nature of Fear

The human body is wired for survival—and separation. At the most primal level, we're alert to danger. We have keen senses that pick up potential threats in the external environment; we have nervous systems primed to react. If the body perceives a risk, the heart races and muscles start firing, making you ready to protect or defend, fight or flee.

What are you protecting? What's really at risk? The life of the separate organism. The fight-or-flight reaction designed to keep the organism alive is incredibly strong. This system works well if you're being chased by a hungry lion; that is, if you genuinely need to protect yourself from physical injury. But when your sophisticated brain gets involved obsessively analyzing every-thing, you're set up to identify as a separate being—and to suffer. To paraphrase Descartes, we think, therefore we believe we exist as separate entities.

Rather than reacting instinctually to the environment as animals do, the fight-or-flight reaction usually doesn't serve a function for us. It keeps us spinning in thought and unable to see things clearly. You feel the body ready to burst into action, then get busy working to interpret, explain, and rationalize what's going on. This is how our capability for sophisticated mental processing goes awry.

You receive a payment-overdue notice from a creditor, and your anxiety surges. Your ex-girlfriend's number shows up on your caller ID, and your body clenches. You lie awake at night, unable to find peace from your thoughts. Or, like many of us, you live with a constant low level of restlessness, which makes being truly happy impossible.

These advanced abilities of the human mind make you conclude that you are the physical body—and that this body of yours is a separate and distinct entity. Then, when you feel fear, you don't just want to protect your physical body, but also your identity. Am I okay? Do I have enough? Am I enough? Am I in danger? With that "I" as a separate identity, you see the world as a scary and uninviting place that threatens your integrity or even your life.

As we've seen in previous chapters, an emotion is a set of physical sensations with a mental story attached. The physical sensations at the core of this instinct to survive are tension, shallow breathing, rapid heart rate, stomach discomfort—all preparing for fight or flight. We know them so well because that's how pervasive the experience of fear is.

Until you see these common sensations for what they are, they prod the mind to analyze, control, and search for solutions. You may not realize it—but every time you notice these physical sensations of a body in danger and thoughts scrambling to protect you from impending doom, fear is driving you.

But you—endlessly magnificent, eternally forgiving—have never been afraid. Yes, you experience fear, but it is in you, not the totality of you. You are aware presence: pure being itself. The experience of fear seems so justified and real—but it is not. When you examine it to its core, you discover no more than the simple arising of sensations and thoughts. You're free—and as you realize that fear is not who you are, you get to consciously experience that freedom. Division melts, and fear completely loses its power.

Yet, the strands of fear run deep. Fear hides out in the most subtle sensations, which often need time and gentle coaxing to be seen. It wends its way into thoughts without your realizing it, descending like a veil over your ability to see clearly. It's the unseen force behind your unsatisfying life choices and behavioral habits.

Here, we thoroughly discuss fear, in order to bring it out of the shadows. Then, you can see how it forms the basis of your personal identity and causes you to feel separate. And you can know it simply as objects that arise in the vast accepting space of you.

When your identity is no longer built on fear, your view expands to reveal endless possibilities. Fear is the guardian of safety and limitation. But, with no entity to defend, protect, or preserve, the perception of fear dissolves into that which is boundlessly alive. This is the province of truth, passion, love, and creative expression in the world.

As you get to know the body and voice of fear in your own experience, you may be surprised to realize how much fear has been in charge. Stay open and curious, and discover the treasure at the heart of fear.

Ways Fear Shows Up

Fear wears many masks. Whenever you look deeply into the reality of human suffering, you'll find fear hiding out—behind the flood of thoughts, inside your tense muscles, in the midst of your edgy mood.

Worry is one of the faces of fear. It's about fear of the unknown, trying to get a sense of control over the unknowable, uncontrollable future. On the surface, you might notice a rush of anxious thoughts. What should I do? What if this happens?

" Whenever you look deeply into the reality of human suffering, you'll find fear hiding out— behind the flood of thoughts, inside your tense muscles, in the midst of your edgy mood."

What if that happens? How can I deal with it? What is she going to say? What if I don't know what to do? How am I going to make it? Although these thoughts surge through the mind, they have no real use. Yet, many of us are caught in chronically worrying, and I was certainly one of them.

Investigating further into the direct experience of worry, you find physical sensations of tension and contraction that you may have never noticed before. This is what we label as fear—scary thoughts about the unknown future, driven by unexplored physical sensations.

Does your mind spin in doubt, hesitation, panic, and dread? Look more deeply at what you feel—and you'll find the physical sensations of fear.

Are you anxious, nervous, stressed, or tense? Yes, fear again!

And if you self-identify as a procrastinator or perfectionist, if you're agitated, shy, or bored, see if fear is driving you.

Fear is at the core of so many patterns that make up the identity of the separate self. It starts with a reactive nervous system whose job is to keep the body safe—then is complicated by a psychological sense that the personal identity is separate and distinct. It seems so real that who you are is a body with an associated identity that needs to be maintained—until you investigate with the light of truth.

The belief that the separate self is real runs deep, and the investigation of this belief highlights this most essential and disconcerting fear. Who are you if not your personal self? Who will you be without it? If you're not the body, what dies? What doesn't?

We are deeply conditioned to avoid what we're afraid of. Yet, if happiness calls you, if your interest in suffering has come to an end, you'll have the courage to look right into the heart of this essential fear that separates you from knowing yourself.

As you see, fear takes many forms. The fear of dissolving the personal self is always at the core, but it usually shows up in more conventional expressions such as worry, doubt, and stress. As you explore the identities that create the belief that you're separate, it serves you to become intimately familiar with how fear speaks and feels. Why? So you can recognize it.

What a discovery this is to see how fear traps you! Once you see it, you can disengage your attention from the rush of thoughts—and notice that sensations appear in awareness. When you know this truth about fear, it stops hooking your attention. You're free to rest as aware presence, free of the power of fear.

Eventually the insight comes: the fear-based identity is false. It doesn't actually define you. You are the aliveness before these thoughts and feelings about fear, and you've never been touched by them. And when you see through the ideas of even time and space, there is just timeless presence. No time for sensations to arise, and no space for them to arise in.

But even this understanding is at risk of being conceptualized by the mind. Let all ideas go, along with all these words trying to describe the indescribable. Know yourself directly as pure, luminous being.

Fear Says, "No!"

You might assume you would know if you're feeling afraid. It's that terror you experience as you're about to step out to speak in front of a crowd. Or the heightened vigilance that comes when you're awakened by an unexpected noise.

But fear can be much more elusive than that. If you're avoiding the physical experience of fear, it shows up in your thoughts. And fearful thoughts are all about "no." Remember that fear tries to protect you and keep you safe—by thinking up all the negative outcomes that could befall you, then convincing you they could happen. Although the bodily sensations of fear happen now, your thoughts *about* fear project into the future you imagine to exist.

"No" used to be my first response to just about everything—a new idea, a suggestion, a request, a possibility. Without even considering it, I'd say "no." For a long time, I didn't realize I was leading with no—and then I didn't get that it was fear-driven. I see it so clearly now, even though this pattern still arises at times. The lack of openness is about keeping control and feeling safe. But these self-imposed limits shield me from so much joyful living!

Fear doesn't want you to leap without knowing the outcome, to live without being on guard, to receive with grace and acceptance. It thrives on certainty: if the future is not known—which, of course, it can never be—it imagines the worst. If you take fear as a central part of your self-definition, you'll be limited in your outlook, your life choices, and in your capacity for sheer joy. You'll be pretending that you're small, when in truth you're immeasurable, pregnant with potential beyond anything imaginable.

Take the thought, "I might fail if I start my own business." If it's not fully examined, this thought could grab you and become your reality. It contains a scary story about an *imagined* negative outcome. If you live in this thought, you'll never start that business. And if you accept the word "fail" when you don't know exactly what failure is, you're closed down, trapped in the negative before you even get going.

Now, imagine you act on an impulse to start a business. Fearful thoughts might arise, but you don't give them attention. You see the "no," but you recognize it as fear and re-center in the space of presence. You stay open and act wisely. You learn as you go, so the word "fail" loses its meaning. You're at ease and efficient. No longer chained down by fear, you can enjoy yourself and respond from love and clarity.

This is the real-life possibility of getting out of your own way by welcoming fear and letting life naturally move you.

The Language of Fear

Fear doesn't always speak directly. If you find yourself alone in a dark alley, you might say, "I'm afraid." But the tentacles of fear are hidden in many thoughts. If the language in your head is peppered with sentences starting with: "I can't," "I shouldn't," "I'd better not," this is fear speaking—trying to protect you from any undue harm. These thoughts project a negative view and support the idea of you as separate from the world.

We've seen that fear speaks the language of "no." It inherently—and diligently—resists the present because it keeps you scanning for threats to your imagined separate self. It holds you back from feeling the freedom of spontaneity and natural being.

Once you stop taking your thoughts at face value and commit to investigating to discover the truth of them, you'll find fear everywhere—at the root of your justifications and rationalizations, behind your ideas about what you're not capable of. It will be there until you see it—and dismantle the power of its spell.

Fear is the building block of self-criticism and doubt. All of these common statements are based in fear:

- I doubt if I can do it.

- I might fail.

- I know they'll disapprove.

- I might get overwhelmed.

- What if I say the wrong thing?

- I have to do it because I can't disappoint her.

- What if I'm criticized?

- I can't go outside my comfort zone.

- What if it gets difficult?

- I don't know how to do it.

You might assume these thoughts help you solve problems, keep control, or organize your experience. But see if this is actually true. If you believe them, no wonder you feel limited and stuck.

Let's apply logic so you can find your way back to peace. First, these thoughts all presume to know what the future will bring—*when you can't actually know.* For example, you think, "What if they disapprove?" But "they" may not even think about it, let alone disapprove of you. Will you fail or become overwhelmed or be criticized? Who knows?

Your thoughts about the future can't reflect reality, and they don't have power to upset you— unless you give them the power. Don't be seduced by the fearful mind, and you are open to what is actually here, living in the unknown because that's what's true.

Now, what about the future that is the subject of so many anxious thoughts? Things happen in the timelessness of aware presence. Even when the mind worries about the future, it does so right now.

"Don't be seduced by the fearful mind, and you are open to what is actually here, living in the unknown because that's what's true."

The future is a creation of the mind: a thought that solidifies the idea of you as a person who needs to stay safe—and distracts you from the brilliance of this now moment. The future is a myth, and presence is effortless, fully alive, and completely trustworthy.

Now that you've busted these fears, who are you? Are you the one thinking these fear-fueled, limiting thoughts—a victim of the imagined negative future? No, that idea no longer makes sense. These thoughts appear, but they aren't about you. They have nothing to do with you, unless you believe they're real and meaningful. Pay no attention to the language of fear, and what remains? You, being, life living itself free of fear.

The Fear Body

We've seen that fearful thoughts don't define you. When you liberate your attention from them, you begin to notice the physical manifestations of fear: tension, clenching, agitation, jitteriness. Let's understand these more deeply.

As some of us know well, certain bodies are sensitive to the sensations of fear. With hardly any provocation, the body reacts as if you just avoided a nasty car accident; your heart races, you contract with tension. If you experience chronic stress and anxiety, these sensations become so familiar that you barely even notice them. But they deserve your attention because they're at the core of your identity as a personal, separate self.

Once you realize that fearful thoughts are unsubstantial and groundless, you can directly experience the physical sensations that have been there all along. Simply be aware as they appear. They may be strong or subtle, concentrated or diffuse. They may change, intensify, or dissolve. Standing as the space in which they arise, you accept them completely, with no goal to feel better or make them disappear. And you allow them to be in presence, over and over, each time they arise.

Awareness meets the deepest physical knots that have been secretly trapped in your body as unexamined sensation. Welcome all of it into awareness like a homecoming. Be concerned only with this moment rather than expecting or hoping for a result. As you let things be just as they are, you stop believing scary stories about fear.

You're merely present, inhabiting this space of unconditional welcoming every time you feel afraid. Without the story, there's only sensation, and the walls of separation dissolve. Layers of fear lodged in the body release. With time, your sensitivity deepens; you notice the fear and experience the sensations before they even have a chance to take hold.

The Physical Contraction of the Separate Self

If you welcome the sensations of fear, you'll likely feel more relaxed and less stressed as patterns unwind. But if you want to be completely at peace, you must directly address the most basic fear: that what you call you—your body—will die. This is the fear at the root of all fears. What you come to realize is that who you are is aware being, prior to all objects, that was never born, never dies, and transcends the sense of yourself as separate.

What keeps you from knowing this is the false sense of "you" who feels the fear of death? Even if you experience all mental conceptions about this "you" as simply thoughts arising and passing on, you still may feel a sense of separation. This sense stems from the belief that your bodily sensations define you as an individual—which distracts you from realizing eternal presence. Eventually, you'll discover a slight contraction, maybe in the chest, behind the eyes, or in your solar plexus. That's your body trying to convince you that you, the person, exist.

This is the origin of all the trouble: this previously unseen subtle sensation that sets in motion a powerful story of you as a separate entity. This is the false identity you've taken to be you.

For me, the sensation was a knot of tension located behind my eyes that I didn't even know existed until it disappeared. When it released, I realized I'd been viewing the world through this compressed tangle of beliefs, shoulds, and expectations. And now there was no filter. It felt like my head had blown open, revealing so much space! There was pure life unfolding, with no personal "me" to control anything, and no distinction between me and any other objects.

A conversation with a friend, dinner with a group of people—all of it was pure intimacy, with nothing separate from anything else. On the face of it, there were people engaging in activities, but the forms were insubstantial, illuminated with presence and vibrating with life.

Continue to open to layers of unexplored sensation. Recognize them as pure experience here in timeless presence. Eventually, everything falls back to its source. You realize the unspeakable, unmoving, undisturbed fullness of reality here, hiding at the heart of the sensation. You aren't located anywhere, and you have no anchor. Yet, you're utterly present and alive, intimate with all.

You're likely to experience deep relaxation in the body. You feel the cells rejoicing in freedom, no longer needing to protect the separate identity. You can finally let go of decades—or eons—of tension, as everything returns to its purely natural state.

Who Dies? What Lives?

As you dismantle the building blocks of the separate self, questions appear. Who dies? What lives? The personal self is made up of two connected ideas—two mental formations: the idea of a body that belongs to you, and the idea of you as an individual with a personal psychology of needs, desires, habits, and preferences—sometimes together called the body-mind.

When you as the separate self say, "I am alive," you assume that the body and the life force that animates it are one and the same—so if the body dies, you die. But this isn't correct. The body is an object; it's not inherently alive.

A potent investigation reveals that there is the body and the life force that animates it. You are the life force. The body is an object that temporarily appears in it. When the body stops being animated—what we call death—has the life force changed? No. It seemed to give life to the body for some time, but the body, by its very nature, won't last. If something appears, it will disappear. And when we attach our survival or contentment to temporary objects such as our body—or someone else's body—we live in fear of their dissolution. The medicine is this: know yourself as the aliveness from which all objects arise, and you are free.

> " When we attach our survival or contentment to temporary objects such as our body or someone else's body we live in fear of their dissolution."

What about the psychological sense of you—the needs, desires, habits, and preferences that seem to be personal to you? When you see them as what they are—objects arising in consciousness—are they you? Can you have none of these but still exist?

Absolutely, yes. These qualities—and the belief in yourself as separate—don't exist without you, awareness, experiencing them. Like all objects, they're impermanent...they arise, change, and disappear. Consciousness is changeless, although change occurs in it. It's deathless, although things appear to die. You are the stable ground of being, pure and awake as life itself.

Knowing this, you feel light, open, and deeply at peace, one with everyone and everything. You're available to the freshness of life in the moment, to joy, creativity, and wonder. No longer trapped by fear or identity, you see people and situations clearly through the eyes of love and compassion. Every moment is known to be precious and tender, not as a platitude, but for real. Nothing may change in your life circumstances, but you perceive everything as if for the first time.

As you see through the illusion of the separate self, fear no longer drives you. All edges soften as you experience everything as connected in a seamless whole. Fearlessness takes over; you grasp that there's nothing to defend, no reason to be vigilant. Habits built on fear lose their hold. They just don't make sense anymore. It's such a relief to let go of all effort, and—just for a moment—not have to sustain the false identity of the separate self.

This is the beginning of truly living. Fear no longer stifles the natural, unconditioned expression of you in the world of form. You're not impeded by worry, doubt, or survival, so every moment is full. You see everything as transparent, overflowing as life itself, a cause for celebration. You're free to revel in the seeming separate self, simply enjoying life and the roles you play.

The mind may be concerned with your ability to function without the fear-based separate entity controlling everything. Returning to the truth of what's real over and over, you effortlessly receive what appears. You think when you need to, plan when it's intelligent to do so, and efficiently manage your responsibilities.

You know you're not the fearful one who says, "No" to life. Finally fearless, you're aware, prone to joy, steeped in love, endlessly generous—living naturally grateful in the deepest acceptance.

Explorations

1. Experiment with being in the unknown. Set aside a morning or afternoon that you keep completely unplanned, with no expectations whatsoever—and let life move you. Be a welcoming presence to any reactions you experience.

2. Get to know how fear speaks in you. Reflect on these questions:

   • What does fear tell you about the future?

   • What does it tell you about yourself and your abilities?

   • If you feel limited in any way, what is fear telling you?

   Now shift your attention away from these thoughts. Recognize that all of this mental activity arises in awareness. What happens if you don't pay attention to these thoughts and rest as simply being aware?

3. Become aware of physical sensations that you label as fear. Let the label go, and experience the sensations directly, as they are.

4. Notice how it takes time for a sensation to arise. The sensation appears, you notice it, it changes or disappears. Experiment with subtracting time. See that there's nothing here—no time or space for a

sensation to take shape. What is your experience? Formless being in the timeless now.

Listen to the guided audio meditation at www.GailBrenner.com/books.

5. Contemplate living without a sense of the separate, defended self. Nothing is separate from anything, including you. You're fearless—because everything is you. Try it on! See what it's like to live in the world without fear. What would you do? How would you feel?

7

Hijacked by Lack and Desire

The problem of inadequacy is rampant in our society. Call it low self-esteem, need for approval, or the disease to please—if you believe in your personal identity, you'll live with the sense that something's missing.

The messages about lack are everywhere. Just watch ten minutes of commercials on TV. You'll be told you aren't young enough or thin enough, or that you don't have the car or even cleaning product you need to be happy. We live in a culture of non-acceptance, which is supported by what many of us learn from our families of origin. We're taught that we're not good enough, that we need exactly what we don't have. It's a legacy of lack.

Of course, this sense of lack seeps into our personal psyches. It might appear like this:

- Living steeped in thoughts about what you should do or be to be acceptable and complete;
- Needing others' approval to feel okay about yourself;
- Constant self-criticism;
- Feeling that there must be something more to life;
- Compulsive behavior that tries to fill your emotional void;

It's like the bucket is always leaking. You rarely feel full, relaxed, and at ease.

And lack breeds desire. If you believe you're missing something, your attention will go out into the world searching for just the right situation, object, or person to finally fulfill you. But even if you get what you think you want, the satisfaction is usually short-lived. How long are you at peace after closing the business deal or finding Mr. Right? Desire traps you in the endless grass-is-always-greener syndrome.

When Lack Is the Driver

Lack and desire are at the root of unhappiness. Feelings of personal inadequacy are so painful—and the stories they tell you about yourself are so demoralizing. The belief that you don't have what you need to be happy, or that you are not enough, is a guarantee that you'll suffer, leaving you struggling to fulfill your needs and desires. In Buddhism, it's called the hungry ghost—that gnawing hunger to seek what you think you're missing but which can never really satisfy.

Though it's uncomfortable to admit, you may be needy for attention and affection. You might feel entitled to get exactly what you think you deserve. You see the world denying you what you desperately need to be whole.

> "The belief that you don't have what you need to be happy, or that you are not enough, is a guarantee that you'll suffer, leaving you struggling to fulfill your needs and desires."

This sense of lack will affect your behavior, as you can't help but bring these cravings into your relationships and daily life. Aiming to please or control others, giving way too much attention to how you present yourself, doing what you feel you have to do but don't really want to—the phantom of lack is behind these behaviors. Inadequacy and desire cloud your judgment, which is why you end up in unsatisfying situations over and over. The hollow grasping blocks out the joy and works against its own fulfillment.

Inadequacy drives your attention out into the world and away from yourself. When you focus on this fragment of conditioning, you forget the true magnificence of you. You search to be filled up as if your life depended on it while neglecting to explore the origin of the problem: the feeling of lack itself.

Freedom from Inadequacy

This exploration offers you the invitation to stop living in "not enough," to stop searching to get what you think you need in order to finally be adequate. Turn your insight into the core of inadequacy to find out if it's true. Realize the possibility that, outside of the sad stories and hopeless feelings, the truth has always been here, waiting to be discovered. You've always been all that you were looking for. You *are* whole and complete, more than enough, full and overflowing—just as you are. You *can* wake up from the dream of personal lack, which is precisely the healing you've been looking for.

As with fear, the threads of lack lie deeply embedded in the idea that you're a limited self. The shortcut to happiness is to separate truth from fiction and live as the endless peace that you are, empty with the light of pure being shining through. But, if you're like most of us, you're entangled in conditioned patterns that drag you along into suffering, even with your best intentions to live in truth.

Learn to recognize the false identity of lack. If left unseen, lack strengthens your identification as separate. And that sets in motion complicated needs, defenses, dynamics, and emotions. You will find lack in the yearning behind loneliness, in the resentment you feel when someone else is chosen, in the despair that makes you cling to or avoid others, in the need to accumulate material objects.

Every experience can be a doorway to freedom from lack. When you feel inadequate, apply your powers of thinking and natural curiosity to discover its truth. Miraculously, simply by investigating, you find that this identity you'd perceived as solid and real is actually transparent—even non-existent. You stop moving into the hook of inadequacy and live as you actually are—nothing needed, nothing missing.

The Effort to Sustain the Separate Self

Although it may not seem so at first, it takes effort to sustain the identity of lack. The mind creates the idea of you as separate from other people. It then compares you with them, or with some idea of how you think you should be, and concludes that you are not enough. It embellishes these stories of inadequacy and looks for evidence to support them—in situations that occur in your life and in the reactions of others. So you search for the love and approval you think will finally make you whole. And you end up believing that something about you is missing or incomplete. It's so complicated! Can you see how you live with blinders on, focusing only on a tiny fraction of reality?

The self-help world tells you that you need to learn to love yourself. But this is not sustainable either. You're taught that if only you would love yourself more, you wouldn't be a victim of your feelings of inadequacy and lack. But who is the you that you're learning to love? Who is doing the loving? And what's this love we're talking about?

"Learning to love yourself" is a strategy fraught with misunderstanding that probably won't help you in the long run. To make it work, you must counteract your thoughts about lack with thoughts about being fulfilled and enough. You must remember to remind yourself that you are complete. Then you must abandon your negative belief system and adopt a more positive one. Rather than *knowing*, in your own experience, that you're whole, you're substituting one identity for another, then working to keep your new, better identity intact. It is all about doing, not being.

The strategy of loving yourself also directs you away from experiencing the physical counterpart of the separate self that needs to be felt—because the sense of separation is inherent to the body. Ignore these sensations and you'll continue to be stuck in inadequacy. But if you look carefully enough, you'll find tension or contraction, a hidden physical holding that's behind the identity as inadequate. Let these sensations be felt so you're less caught up in the belief that you're incomplete and lacking, leaving you free to notice the ever-presence of simply being.

The only true solution to lack is to realize that the story isn't about you. It isn't even personal to you. It's merely mental chatter appearing in consciousness—and it doesn't relate to the essence of you no matter how strongly you may feel in any moment that it does.

When you realize, through deep investigation into the absolute truth, that you've always been here and alive prior to these thoughts, you release your attention from this debilitating story. Then you have the space to be fully aware. What do you notice? What you thought was inadequacy turns out to be thoughts and physical sensations arising in consciousness. As you rest in awareness and let everything be, the identity as inadequate begins to unravel. You stop wasting this precious life ensnarled in the false identity that you're not enough and that you have to *do* more to *be* more. You start truly living.

These stories of inadequacy and the desire they create run deep in the belief of human separation. Become an expert in how they work in you so you can begin to live as who you really are—expansive and free. Continually investigate to know the truth of your in-the-moment experience. This courageous exploration wears away these habits, just as wind and waves gently turn rock into sand.

Inflated and Deflated Self-Identities

The seed of inadequacy leads you to personal stories of either inflation or deflation. You think of yourself as less-than or better-than. You either undervalue or overvalue yourself—two sides of the same coin. In both, you're comparing yourself to others or to some imaginary ideal in your mind. It's a thought-based tendency that eclipses the reality of presence shining through everything.

The pain of deflation knows no bounds. If you nurture the secrets of personal shame and inadequacy, if you believe that you're damaged, in need of repair, or missing a piece that can make you whole—you're living in deflation. The inner language of deflation can be so harsh—calling yourself a loser, no good, or worse. No wonder you feel depressed and lonely. Fearing rejection and craving love, you understandably compromise yourself by making life choices that minister to your insecurities rather than your pure heart. It's a painful existence to live in yearning and not having.

What underlies inflation is similar, but the expression is different. Pride, arrogance, entitlement, narcissism, feeling special, striving for control and dominance—these are the false identities of the inflated separate self. You think that you deserve to be treated in a particular way or that you're entitled to certain outcomes. These patterns act as a shield, masking the fundamental sense of self-doubt that gives rise to them.

The core of this identity goes far back in time. Where do you learn that you're less than whole, that you need to be filled up? You somehow absorbed this message in childhood. As children we're vulnerable to what happens around us. We view the world from a self-centered perspective, primed to think we're at fault or to blame for whatever losses we suffer.

For example, if you regularly experienced rejection as a child, you might reasonably assume it's because you're unworthy. Why else would a parent reject you? Of course, there are many other reasons having to do with your parent's own confusion, but the young mind is rarely capable of perceiving them. This self-identification as unworthy feeds a persistent longing for the love and acceptance you were denied. And this longing generates the deflated and inflated personal identities, based on a belief in lack.

Then life becomes a self-fulfilling prophecy. If you view the world through the lens of inadequacy, you might choose a dominating partner. Then you wonder why you're always taken advantage of. Or you inhibit your creative expression for fear of negative judgment—and complain that you're unfulfilled. Those with inflated identities experience many interpersonal problems. You might maintain your fragile sense of self by putting people down and indulging in other behaviors that sustain your exaggerated self-importance.

Both presentations contain the seed of desire. You long to find what you perceive as missing. This belief motivates endless seeking for love, power, money, recognition, and material objects—based on the mistaken assumption of personal lack.

No matter how convincing these stories might be, neither identity is the truth of you. How could it be? It consists of congealed mental and emotional forms that appear in presence. Being aware, you know that they're the result of conditioning, and they're not real.

Question this story—don't take it at face value. Are you actually inadequate or the one entitled to have things your way? Who is it who believes this?

Whenever these beliefs, urges, and feelings arise, take a breath and let your mind open like a cloudless sky. Shift your attention to this space, and already what seems to be real begins to soften. Stay unengaged with these objects and they're free to come and to go. As you recognize the expansion into conscious presence, these meaningless experiences lose their capacity to seduce you into feeling that there's something wrong with you. Your natural intelligence invites you to stop believing them. You seriously entertain the possibility that you're already complete, just as you are.

> " *Whenever these beliefs, urges, and feelings arise, take a breath and let your mind open like a cloudless sky. Shift your attention to this space, and already what seems to be real begins to soften.* "

As you let the stories fall away, you have space to perceive the underlying sensations. These may feel dull, dark, heavy, or empty. Allow them to be, without doing anything. Each time you notice the arising of the inflated or deflated identity, disconnect with the story and welcome your direct experience of the sensations in loving openness. Then *be* the loving openness.

I remember a time when I felt arrogant because I thought I should have been recognized for my abilities and experience when I wasn't. The feeling came up like a fire. I let go of the story in my mind and opened to intense physical sensations. For the first time ever, I noticed the burn behind the feelings of entitlement and wanting to be right. It was humbling to begin with, but ultimately a huge relief to be liberated from this painful hook.

When you meet all reactions as they are, you dispel them before they have a chance to grab hold. You return to aware presence, the stillness of you. Not the false, created, wounded you, but the purity of you, true and alive.

In that state, no thoughts or emotions—or any other objects—have the space or time to be constructed. They give way to the recognition of formless reality. And here's the treasure: what you thought was empty or lacking turns out to be completely full.

Everywhere you look, at the heart of everything, you see life—endlessly intimate and inseparable from you. The old habit of pining for love becomes a joke—simply an idea that has no basis in reality. Because you know that reality—in its pure state, free of form—is abundantly generous, just as it is, because it contains everything. Compassion might arise toward the illusion of the confused one who believed something was missing as the truth reveals that you were always complete, whole, inclusive of all.

Long-standing patterns of an inadequate self-identity take time to unwind, even if the separate self has dissolved and you know your true nature. You might be frustrated when conditioning seems to reappear because you want your experience of peace to be stable. Rather than feeding another mind-created story that tells you that you aren't aware enough or blames you for the shift of attention back into an old habit, let it be. In truth, you can't move one millimeter away from yourself, although the mind may convince you otherwise. Once you recognize that attention has been drawn into the mind—another beautiful moment of awakening—shift to being aware. Effortlessly, without drama, disengage from all thoughts, and recognize pure being. Each shift untangles the conditioned false identity a little bit more.

Notice how the experience of being is different from gripping onto the beliefs about lack and inadequacy. Where you'd thought you were incomplete, is anything actually lacking? Are there any boundaries? Is anything not included? What about needing love from someone else to feel okay about yourself? In being, there is no you-and-other. Edges disappear, and fullness is known, alive everywhere.

Not Taking Things Personally

If you feel a sense of lack, you're taking things personally. Someone says or does something, and you, believing you are separate, take it as personal to you. In both the deflated and inflated identities, an emotional reaction results from feeling rejected, disregarded, or criticized. How is it possible to be free of this torment? Can you imagine being finished with the drama of exclaiming, "I can't believe he did that to me!" or suffering in silence as you tend your wounds?

The experience of hurt feelings involves a host of complicated dynamics. First, you define yourself by the sense that something in you is missing, wrong, or not good enough. Then, you live in the constant craving for love and approval. This makes you sensitive to how others respond to you and sets the stage to take things personally. Any insult or perceived rejection seems to confirm your worst fears about yourself—that you are unworthy and unlovable—and you feel hurt.

The starting point to untangle this web is to recognize the stories you tell. What he said, how you felt, your indignation— these emotion-laden thoughts cycle around in your mind, causing you pain. Although you may have lived these thoughts as your reality for a long time, you now know that they're just like any other thought—just mental chatter made up of false content. They have meaning only if you think they're true. And if you do, the power of your belief gives them power over you.

Understanding the nature of these thoughts is your ticket to freedom—because they're distorted and inaccurate. Once you no longer buy into the story of insufficient you, you're open to emerging from the web of suffering. Sensations may come into presence, and you let them be. Resting your attention in awareness, you notice space…and peace.

As you work with this constellation of thoughts and feelings over time, it begins to subside. No longer attached to the identity of inadequacy, you barely react, leaving space for insights to appear. You stop resisting reality. Instead of saying, "I'm so hurt because he did that," you relax and you accept what happened. Then you can inquire:

- What motivated him to do that? Maybe he's caught in confusion or suffering.

- What got triggered in me? I'm curious about that.

- Is he treating me the way I treat myself?

- Can I respond from wholeness, not lack?

- What's the essential truth of this moment?

These questions help to break through the trap of identification as unworthy. But they're stepping-stones to the ultimate understanding. When you don't believe in the idea of a you who's lacking and capable of being hurt, there's nowhere for any attack or unkind comment to land. From the perspective of absolute reality, you might hear sounds. But they're someone else's story and have no meaning as your attention rests in the knowing of limitless awareness.

Say that your partner criticizes the way you handled a situation at work. If you react from the separate self, you'll close up—feeling hurt, defensive, and angry. You'll be primed to argue or isolate yourself. But with no personal identity to protect, you take a breath. You stay open and curious. You're present with your experience, rather than resisting it. You take the time to listen deeply. In the most natural way, you stay connected, loving, and respectful. And you explore whether there is something of value to learn from the critique—perhaps about your behavior, your reaction to your partner's assessment, or your partner's current state of mind.

We typically think that when we take things personally, we feel hurt by what someone else says or does. But "taking things personally" can mean using someone else's words or action as weapons against oneself—as proof of the inadequacy we have come to believe defines us. It has another meaning in the inflated identity. Boasting, feeling entitled or deserving, being puffed up by success, recognition, or fame—this is the separate self taking credit where credit is not due.

Creativity is expressed so beautifully in the world—in art, music, dance, film, architecture, science, writing. But these expressions aren't personal to any individuals, no matter how talented they seem. These are forms that first appear in consciousness as ideas or urges, then are manifested through intelligent action. For example, a melody and lyrics appear, and the songwriter sits down with pen or instrument in hand and brings them to fruition as a song. She might even become famous for her creations. And she may build a solid identity around being a well-known artist. But still, in truth, there's no one to take credit, no one responsible—only appearances in awareness that tell an enjoyable story. This is the nature of creativity.

Any skill or talent you possess comes through you, but it is not you. If you take it personally, thinking you're special because of its presence, you'll use it to strengthen your idea of yourself as a separate person. But if you celebrate it as a joyful arising without identifying with it, you allow it to be expressed in ways you can't possibly know or plan. Your personal conditioning is out of the way, leaving an open channel for the life force to be freely expressed through you.

Attaching to delightful qualities or successful outcomes to support the inflated identity is like building a house on sand. In fact, it takes great effort to maintain this version of separation. When you define yourself by something that is temporary, or when you look to the world for happiness, you set yourself up for a fall. No matter how amazing your life circumstances, they can't last because they're not truly real. What to do? Enjoy yourself to the hilt in the play that arises, but remember that it isn't who you are.

Stay the Course

The identities that develop around lack, inadequacy, and self-importance can be very sticky. Their tentacles run deep into the very heart of your self-image, and they've likely been wending their way through you for most of your life. This means that unwinding them takes time.

Even if you have the best intentions not to feed these stories, the momentum of conditioning takes over—and you find yourself believing them once again. Your job is to be with the full humanity of emotional experiences that arise as you live in the world. This is what chips away at these compelling patterns.

Be fierce in your investigation of how you make yourself appear to be separate—and be tender in allowing space for these habits to unravel. Rejoice every time you realize that the identity has taken hold—because this is awareness welcoming you home. If your fire for the truth is unwavering, these moments add up.

One day, you'll realize that what used to bother you rarely does anymore. Or you'll notice that, miraculously, a new response to an old trigger appears. For example, you're willing to say "no" rather than bend to others' wishes. Or you allow a creative idea to take shape rather than rationalizing why you should ignore it. You notice moments of peace where there'd been pain before. And sometimes you find that you're happy for no apparent reason.

When you find it difficult to disengage from the story of lack, try "acting as if." Pretend you're free of these limiting beliefs, completely full, not missing or desiring anything. Play with seeing everything as yourself. Imagine yourself—and everything else—so saturated with love that it can't be contained. How would that feel in your mind and in your body? What would you think—or do?

> " When you find it difficult to disengage from the story of lack, "act as if." Pretend you're free of these limiting beliefs, completely full, not missing or desiring anything."

Every moment of awareness counts. It takes only a simple movement of attention away from objects and back to being aware. Here is the possibility of happiness. Skipping over nothing, you feel the pain of deficiency, and it reveals unending fullness. Burning in pride gives way to the magic and relief of ordinariness. Give it time and your heartfelt attention, be willing to be nothing, and discover the unlimited nature of you.

What Now?

What comes after these familiar false friends of lack, need, and not enough? If you don't spend your time and energy trying to seek love and avoid rejection, if you no longer feel compelled to nurse your wounds—what *do* you do?

The world may start to look very different to you. You may wonder: How do I function? How will I know what to do? What will happen to my relationships? To my life?

You can function very well without the mind's invention of a separate self, but you won't trust this until you know it in your own experience. Look at how you get through your day. You might find thoughts that seem to guide and organize you. But when you subtract the thinking, you'll see that the life stream of presence is always here. You eat, drive, clean, smile, breathe, and hug—all of this unfolds effortlessly. Think about what happens when you have a conversation with someone. Can you possibly know and plan every word that comes out of your mouth? A flow of experience simply occurs, powered by natural intelligence.

As the habits that make up the separate self dissolve, you realize that life is. When you live here, you're in constant surrender. You're so willing to know yourself as the totality that the babbling mind doesn't affect you. What was once your agitated mental space is clear and open, even when thoughts appear. And when thoughts are needed, they arise. You can balance your checkbook or shop for ingredients and a make a delicious pie. Your body moves. You take care of your children. You're responsible in your life.

In the complete surrendering of the mind, you enter the world of the unknown. In fact, things were always unknown. No matter how much you deliberated and planned, you never knew what you were going to do until it actually happened. But now, you're aligned with the unfolding—you *are* the unfolding.

To put it another way, you don't decide the next thing; it just happens. Your personality doesn't disappear entirely. You still have preferences, an age, a gender, and personal characteristics—but you hold it all lightly. It's just like acting in a play. You play the part of you as a separate self, but you fully know that it isn't real.

And when you no longer believe your personal identity, you are clear about your life circumstances. Seeing through the eyes of non-separate reality, you're compassionate and unafraid. Taking fear out of the equation leaves you open to seeing that your relationships may have been built on mutual need, that your life choices were made to protect and defend. Realizing this, actual changes in your life situation may, or may not, occur. But it's not for you to know. The totality of life takes care of all of it perfectly. The personal self is not required.

Once you're no longer driven by thought, the body becomes a guide. Physical sensation is a sensitive barometer that reacts to shifting circumstances. When in doubt, check in with the body. In any moment, if you open to the whole of your experience, clarity emerges from the clouds.

And oh, the peace, the joy! Every moment so tender, bursting with life, overflowing with potential. You revel in delight and wonder. Gratitude is boundless. You feel deeply, with no residue. But none of that is your business. Discover the truth of you, and all will be revealed.

Explorations

1. Know in your heart of hearts that you lack nothing. Any story about being wounded, broken, or not good enough is simply not true. As these stories arise, stop engaging with them. Keep returning to presence, over and over.

2. Reflect on the ways you behave that don't serve you. Can you see how these patterns are driven by a sense of lack?

   Take away the content of the story, and feel the sensations in your body, just as they appear. Let them come out of hiding! Meet them with the deepest acceptance.

3. Recognize that you're aware, and stand squarely as awareness.
   - Is awareness bothered by any story?
   - When you stand as awareness, is anything lacking?

   This is who you really are.

4. When you feel hurt, insulted, or rejected, challenge the story that grips you. Know that it doesn't actually define who you are. Lose interest in the story, and directly experience what remains. Be present as the timeless now for whatever arises.

Listen to the guided audio meditation at
www.GailBrenner.com/books.

8

Awake in Relationship

As the saying goes, if you think you're enlightened, go spend time with your family. Relationship is right where the rubber meets the road. The dynamics in relationship reveal the remnants of belief in the personal self and highlight the pain of living as if conditioned reactions were true. And relationship is the mirror that offers the invitation to embrace and see through the triggers that sabotage your happiness so you can know the peace that you are.

From the perspective of pure reality, there's no thing called a relationship. There's only being, with no two people existing independently to be in relationship with one another. But the form of relationship as it appears in the world—and in your life—is so incredibly rich. We get to feel the human experience of emotions and discover how they can bring us closer—and drive us apart. It's joyful to celebrate the play of forms together. And when you realize that nothing is separate from anything else, there's only tenderness, and intimacy beyond words.

You may not realize it, but you already know non-separation. At the core of the human experience of love, gratitude, caring, true friendship, or union, you've tasted the truth of you. It's what lies behind any division or distance. You feel moved to help a stranger or pour out generosity to a friend. You weep when you see the suffering of people half a world away. These human responses arise spontaneously from the one heart.

In relationships that are not confused by strategies and dynamics, love simply is. What you love about the "other" isn't the form of the person or their conditioning. In fact, most people's conditioning isn't inherently lovable.

But when form and conditioning are known to be transparent, the essence of the formless shines through. This is the spontaneous recognition of the one Self, the place where two meet—and dissolve into the totality. The other doesn't complete you or make you feel whole—these ideas are in the territory of the separate self. Rather, you realize the wholeness that you already are, which includes the apparent "other."

Distorted Beliefs in Relationship

So often, we confuse need with love. When you take yourself to be a separate entity, your connections with others are built upon a desire for fulfillment, fear of rejection or being alone, or need for love, acceptance, or control. You're left living in lack and dissatisfaction. Either you focus on molding yourself into what you think others want or you become a master at distancing and avoidance. Your attention is drawn into the world as you try to figure out how to manage the hole you feel, and the mind is set in motion—judging, analyzing, and ruminating.

> "The trouble in relationship starts with the belief in separation—that you're an individual with a personal self, relating to other individual, personal selves."

The trouble in relationship starts with the belief in separation—that you're an individual with a personal self, relating to other individual, personal selves. Then, from your island, you project onto others your beliefs, fears, and desires: "I should be married"…"I'm afraid of getting rejected"…"family gatherings should be fun"…"my children should be successful"…"you're not doing it right."

Beliefs like these create expectations that are bound to leave you disappointed. They keep you trying to figure out how to get what you think you want and need.

The results?

- Trying to control other people and feeling resentful when you realize you can't.

- All kinds of relationship drama.

- Endless gossip about who did what to whom.

- Innocent children affected by families falling apart.

Your attention is pulled into the objects of the world, while happiness and peace seem unattainable.

These beliefs take the unfolding of a moment that's fresh and alive—and box it in with demands and expectations. They attempt to give structure to something that's wildly free of structure. And they give rise to feelings that seem hard to manage.

A friend wrote of her intense frustration at continuing to snap at her husband and raise her voice with her children. She was full of beliefs about what her loved ones should and shouldn't do, how she failed herself, how her relationship with her husband should be different. She was very wound up, and her suffering was palpable. She could recognize that she held these beliefs, but couldn't find release from them.

She didn't realize how intently she was comparing what she thought she wanted with how things actually were. And, as we know, stories of comparison always conclude that something's missing or not right. No wonder she was so frustrated!

The conventional way of addressing this common problem is to help her understand that she's probably projecting beliefs from her own childhood experiences onto her family to try to heal those early relationships, and to offer her skills to handle her emotions. These approaches may help for some time, but don't get to the core of the problem.

The true resolution comes when you recognize the beliefs as they occur in the moment and choose to *turn away from them.* Then you become available to the field of presence that lovingly welcomes your emotional reactions and the accompanying physical sensations—and you can let them be. Rather than being stuck, you're open to the possibility of insight and clear seeing.

Is taking a belief to be true creating confusion and disharmony in your relationships? Investigate to see:

- Is it true?

- Is it aligned with what's actually happening?

- Does it serve peace and happiness?

Then see the belief as merely mental chatter. Give no attention at all to its content. Stop, take a breath, and return your attention to just being, directly experiencing any feelings that arise.

The mind is likely to put up a fight. "Of course he should take out the trash!" it says. Your job is to open to the righteous burn of feeling justified in your resentment and to any other emotion that appears. Is it true that he should take out the trash? No. That's your fabricated idea of how things are supposed to be, an argument with truth. What's true is that he doesn't do it.

Disengage from this thinking, and worlds open up. You feel what's actually here! You're available to new perspectives on the situation and potentially new ways of handling it. Maybe you willingly take out the trash because it's there to be done—or you don't. Maybe you ask genuine, heartfelt questions. Maybe a long-overdue honest conversation finally has the space to happen. See how every moment offers an opportunity for freedom?

When you abandon your beliefs about how things should be in your relationships, you give up expecting anything from anyone. You're free to see clearly without the veils of fear and lack. You receive emotions—your own and others'—in ways that don't cloud your thinking. Giving up what you thought you knew, you arrive in the land of the unknown, not knowing what will happen or how you will respond.

You show up fresh in the moment without layers of history. You see and feel others as if for the first time—because it *is* the first time in this moment. Interactions that had been stuck take on a new light. Rather than closing down into same-old-same-old, you're open and vulnerable; you lead with a compassionate heart. Mind-created limits collapse, giving way to new insights and creative ways of responding. What was frozen is now free.

If you find yourself in a familiar reaction or participating in a conversation as if you're repeating the lines of a script you've said many times, you're caught in a conditioned habit. Follow the breadcrumbs back to the truth—to awareness that is the one heart, yourself in all forms, including the one in front of you who you think is causing the problem. Put down your arms and end the war—with your own experience. Stop and breathe, and fully allow your feelings to be.

Understanding the deepest truths about reality isn't abstract or airy-fairy. It's practical and applies directly to real-world situations. Even though you've had a taste of the peaceful nature of non-separate reality, your life stream, the wave of you in the vastness of the ocean, still comes through a body, and you function in the world. You might even be more engaged, because you respond to the direct experience of what's right in front of you—no longer masked by complex dynamics and belief systems. You don't live in your head—you truly live, finally fully human. It's an everyday miracle.

The world of relationship comes alive. Your experience is so fresh. You don't need to strategize about what to do or say; the appropriate response arises naturally. You're free to love without limit and care until your heart breaks open, over and over. But you're not a doormat or pushover. The natural intelligence that moves through you knows when to say "no," when enough is enough, when you need to go. The clarity shines like a beacon.

The Futility of Survival Strategies

As separate body-minds, we're in relationship even before we're born. When you were developing in the womb, you were sensitive to sounds, stress, and the health and lifestyle of your mother. Then, you were born into a family, and had to rely on others for your basic needs for the first several years of life. Virtually all your conditioned habits and tendencies evolved out of these very early relationships—because they were critical to your development, but rarely completely fulfilling.

Although parents do their best, you may have been left feeling judged, neglected, or unloved. If these experiences become part of your identity, some of your relationships are bound to be complicated. You see yourself and others through the film of conditioning and not with the clarity of the unconditioned you.

As we grow up, we accept the false logic that we're separate selves relating to other separate selves. We're driven by fear and lack, projecting these uncomfortable states onto others so we don't have to feel them. And we feel compelled to play out interpersonal strategies that ultimately leave us alienated and dissatisfied. These dynamics most often occur outside of conscious awareness, but the thinking goes like this:

- I'm inadequate—so, to feel okay about myself, I need to do what it takes to be liked by the people around me.

- I need to cling to people out of fear of being alone.

- I need to be pushy and aggressive to maintain control.

- If I keep my distance, I'll be safe.

- I have a right to have others meet my needs.

We tend to move toward, away, or against others—toward them to seek approval and connection, away out of fear of closeness and exposure, or against to dominate and preserve control. These highly conditioned strategies have peace as their goal—but they're built on distorted ideas that solidify the false sense of separation in which there can never be peace.

Unless you're one of the blessed few, it doesn't dawn on you to look anywhere but outside yourself for happiness and peace. After all, that's what you did as a small child. And that's what everyone around you is doing—living in a collective dream, imagining that happiness is not here in this moment, and hoping that it can be found through fulfilling interactions with others.

" That's what everyone around you is doing—living in a collective dream, imagining that happiness is not here in this moment, and hoping that it can be found through fulfilling interactions with others."

But at some point, you realize that continuing your search for happiness will only keep you locked into the act of searching—it won't actually get you what you're searching for. In fact, ongoing distress and dissatisfaction are a clear sign that you're waiting for happiness to come to you from others—and you're not considering that it's already present. You think there must be another way. And there is.

It's a matter of giving up the search for something outside yourself and turning your attention inward. Rather than looking to your relationships to satisfy your needs, make you whole, and take away your fears, you see that these stories make you believe you want what's not here.

Then, the blinders come off. Seeing through the eyes of truth, you realize that fulfillment isn't found by avoiding your experience. It's here right at the core of fear and lack.

Fear is energy, and lack is experienced as a hole or a heaviness in the chest or belly. When you embrace these feelings fully, you see that they arise in perfect harmony, inseparable from you being aware, inseparable from the timeless now. You know there's no separate entity who experiences these feelings. They're not personal to you, only sensations arising in consciousness.

Needs, fears, loss, rejection, control, isolation, conflicts around intimacy—these are all the province of the personal identity. They originate from conditioning and create endless complicated interactions in relationships. But when we fully meet our emotions, the clouds part. Relationship becomes what it was always meant to be: joyful celebration. The potential to end the search—along with the longing and desire—is always here; know that you can start at any moment.

Non-Separate Living in Relationship

Most of us don't live in an altered state of bliss, like a monk on a mountaintop. Yes, reality is the seamless, formless unfolding of experience. But within this infinite totality, forms appear. Released from the prison of a personal identity comprised of habits, you're free to enjoy yourself in everyday life. The world becomes a playground, free of resistance. You begin to experience needing, getting, and protecting as irrelevant. Doing gives way to being. Love overflows unfiltered—how could it not? And you know in the moment just how to respond to people and situations. And if you don't, your responses are measured, not impulsive, with no fear of being still.

Relationships transform as the barriers created by identification collapse. Say you experience conflict in your relationship with your child because his interests don't match your vision of what his life should look like. Or maybe you hold a grudge against your parents for events that happened long ago—and still relate to them through these unexamined emotions. Or perhaps you live in a world of "should"—making your peace dependent on what others do or say—only to feel frustrated when these expectations clash with reality.

Seeing through these belief systems leaves you free of suffering and opens you to participate in relationships without being triggered. You guide your child wisely and lovingly, while supporting his natural inclinations. You approach your interactions with your parents with a freshness that sparkles, rather than through the veils of resentment. You simply receive what happens as it is, instead of experiencing friction when things don't go as you wish them to. You have no agenda or ax to grind.

In relationships experienced from the perspective of truth and wholeness, you flow with ease. This doesn't mean that challenges don't arise. But they're met with openness and clear seeing. Differences of opinion will happen—but since you no longer strive to sustain a personal identity, you hold your positions lightly. Expectations of others, which can subtly erode your relationships, are seen through. You don't need to be right or take things personally. Rather, you're flexible, open, and curious—moving *with* what's happening rather than against it.

This doesn't mean that you won't react. Relationship is the great fertile ground to discover any remaining conditioning. Conditioned reactions will arise, and when they do, you can inquire into the truth of them rather than act from them. Disengage from the content of confusing beliefs, and welcome all hidden emotions you experience in your body with a full and open heart.

If you find yourself recycling a stream of thoughts or behaving to please, avoid, oppose, or control—a habit has taken hold, maybe with great intensity. You'll experience the pain of feeling alienated from others. Let the force of the habit unwind. As you allow what is happening in your mind and body, what was stuck becomes free. You replace automatic momentum with alert stillness. Your contracted mind reveals unlimited openness. Now you can be truly intimate with "others."

Every moment offers the possibility of a doorway to awaken to the truth of yourself. Experiment by showing up freshly as you interact with someone familiar to you. Forget everything you know, everything that has happened in the past, all your opinions and desires, and rest in the fullness of aware presence. Listen deeply, with nothing in the way. Be transparent and accepting, and trust in the insights and responses that arise naturally in you.

The Essential Relationship Skill

Relationships exist in your life to support you in unraveling from your own conditioning. If you want to show up free and unencumbered with others, be willing to go beyond the conventional methods of self-help to improve communication or air your feelings. Take full responsibility for the reactions that arise within you in your relationships. You might want to blame, project, analyze, control, fix, hide, or passively hope for change. But as you inquire into these reactions rather than acting them out, your attention shifts inward to meet your own experience, even in trying situations.

Eventually, the momentum of these reactive tendencies dies down—a lot. By welcoming your in-the-moment experience, you stop dancing your version of the relationship dance. The dynamic you recycle with others comes to a halt because you've stopped your role in it. You'll find tremendous freedom for new ways of being.

I learned this first-hand after years of relationship stress. I believed that I was supposed to communicate by sharing my feelings and concerns with my partner. It was miraculous to realize that when I simply experienced feelings and bodily sensations first, they dissipated along with the need to have "the talk." Upset transformed into empty space. The need to be heard yielded to stillness. I definitely became kinder.

The mind-made stories lost their power. And with nothing in the way, there was room for love, openness, and the joys of ordinary life.

The primary work of relationship is neither to improve communication nor to negotiate conflicting needs. It's deeper than that. When you open to include everything, you're no longer constricted by beliefs. You are available to meet your reactions with loving presence.

And when you do, you stop wreaking havoc in your relationships through unchecked emotional drama. Interactions are clean, with no subtext, no underlying intention to get, resist, or avoid. You're openhearted, free to respond as needed.

As you shift your attention to rest in pure being, your thoughts and feelings seem less solid. Any action comes naturally, impersonally, without any mediation from the imagined separate self. You realize that the distinction you perceive between you and others is false. Division collapses, and only true love remains. This is the living reality of what's possible.

Intimate Relationship

Your relationship with your partner offers a beautiful laboratory that supports your awakening. When you live with someone day in and day out, it's nearly impossible to hide. You *will* express your conditioned programming because it's dug in deep.

> " *Your relationship with your partner offers a beautiful laboratory that supports your awakening.*"

Finally, as you turn your attention inward, you recognize the choice available in every moment. Unless you admit to conditioned patterns, you'll live in self-betrayal, play unspoken games of withholding and cruelty, or collude with your partner to keep the truth at bay so you don't rock the boat. These strategies create painful experiences within yourself and in your relationship and keep your personal identity intact.

This way of being in a long-standing relationship may seem so normal that it doesn't feel like a choice—but it is. And you can choose not to join with the vast majority of partners who tacitly agree to make do. You can break the unexpressed pact to maintain the status quo, even if this level of honesty feels threatening. It becomes more important to be true than to continue betraying yourself.

With the full commitment to ending resistance and seeing things as they actually are, your relationship becomes an unobstructed window into your habitual ways of being. Rather than staying entangled in stories and reactions, you have the opportunity to illuminate the truth of your experience.

This investigation is yours and takes place in your own heart-mind space, although it can be beautifully shared when there are two willing partners. As you become clearer about the roles you've been adopting and the strategies you both play out, it's so tempting to start finding fault with the other. After all, *you've* seen the light. If blaming thoughts worm their way into your mind, don't indulge them. Keep your focus on untangling your own conditioned habits.

The desire for freedom involves seeing through all attachments—even to your partner. Finally, in fierce acceptance of the ways you've been asleep in your relationship, you become willing to leave your comfort zone. You can no longer join in unsatisfying or damaging dynamics. You show up fresh, ready to know the truth.

By seeing yourself and your partner clearly, through wide-open eyes, anything can happen. You might fall silent in deep acceptance or begin to speak authentically, even though it's scary. There may be renewed connection, deeper intimacy and understanding, clarity about how to move forward in truth. The end of well-worn habits you mutually play out signals release from identities that limit you and your relationship. The belief in separation yields to deep self-recognition, where the boundaries between you and your partner are transparent, and you meet in pure presence.

Don't be deterred if your partner shows no interest in truthful investigation and communion in intimacy. Follow your own heart, and walk your own path. It's ultimately a solo journey anyway. Do it without reservation, and everything will be revealed.

The Conundrum of Attachment

In the world of separation, it's easy to become attached. Believing you're a separate, personal identity, there is always a sense that something's missing, along with the hope that you'll finally be fulfilled through relationship.

When you're attached to someone, you're trying to feel secure. You want your partner to stay with you forever (or you want one to appear), you don't want your children to grow up, you expect those close to you to do what you want them to do. You want your relationships to be different, or you want them to stay the same. Yet, what happens has nothing to do with your personal desires. And when you want something different than what appears, you suffer. Looking at the facts, it's folly to be attached to wanting anything from your relationships and wisdom to rest in things as they are.

Suppose you expect your manager to praise you for a job well done, but she doesn't. You're attached to wanting acknowledgment—but you didn't receive it. You might obsess about this situation in your mind, feel sad or angry, and judge your manager's behavior. And you might experience stress, running on to co-workers or family members about your dissatisfaction. All this strain comes from being attached to specific outcomes in this relationship.

You're caught in personal identification, believing thoughts that tell you what should happen, and even justifying them. Meanwhile, you're avoiding your feelings. How do you show up in relationships when you're attached to what happens? Scared, needy, and dissatisfied.

Wanting and attachment are integral to the separate self, rooted in history, habit, and fear. No matter how reasonable it sounds, it's not enough to say, "Don't be attached to outcomes." Instead, dispel the attachment with loving, laser-like inquiry:

- What's my direct experience of being attached?

- What are its effects?

- Is fear present?

- Who is the one who is attached?

This line of questioning will show you that feeling attached pulls your attention into the black hole of believing you're separate. And these reflections invite the stable ground of presence to come into view. Rediscover the truth of you—not the mind-created limited you. Attachments to others in relationship will no longer have a place. You know with great clarity that you don't need or lack anything, and these attachments untangle quite naturally.

In the freedom of not knowing, you'll stop being concerned about what others think of you. You won't need your strategies to get love and approval anymore. Where you used to cling, you'll stay centered in yourself. With the release from need and fear, some relationships may fall away—and others will flourish in truth and clarity. As you notice your tendencies to attach but don't act on them, you'll skillfully navigate the terrain of relationship, while remaining clear and openhearted.

Let's return to the problem with your manager. Put every single belief aside—including the idea of you as a personal self—and view the situation from aware presence that needs nothing. Allow your feelings to be as they are. Where does that leave you? Instead of buying into stories about your need for praise, you know you're already complete. You approach your manager with openness—seeing her fears and her essential wholeness. Because you're no longer attached to changing her behavior, your resistance falls away, making space for a new kind of interaction. You do your work for the sake of doing it and not for praise and recognition. You no longer need to think and talk about the situation; you're free of its grip. You flow like water.

Just for a moment, imagine being free of attachments to people and situations. Things come and go, but you're stable and unmoving in the midst of it all. It doesn't mean you don't care. In fact, as clinging subsides, you're finally open to real, unconditioned love. On the surface, you experience communion with "others," but in truth you've tapped into the overflowing nature of non-separate awareness. Knowing there is no other, you only experience yourself—not your separate self, but the essence of you, which is seen as the essence of everything. Attachment and need are the food of separation. The end of attachments reveals the most intimate state of being.

In the world of forms, attachment creates the inevitability of loss. While you're busy trying to get your personal needs met, you overlook the tender fact that no forms last. Anything that appears will eventually disappear, including your partner, your children, your parents, your friends, yourself, and all your possessions.

Yet, is the goal really not to be attached? Don't you form attachments to a child born with your DNA or loved as family from birth? Don't you feel attached to your partner through sexual union and deep, long-term companionship, which can create the closest of friendships? Even with the most profound realization of non-separation and complete disloyalty to thoughts, you may be afraid of change, absence, and loss.

Look around you. Everything and everyone you encounter will go. If it appeared at some point in time, it will disappear. This is the nature of forms. Once you understand this, you feel deeply, but you don't cling or hide…you revel in the play of relationships, even though you know you're not separate. This recognition invites the sweetest surrender into love.

Nothing is a problem unless you make it into one with a troubling or dramatic story. Meet your attachments directly to break through the fear of losing people you love. And when they leave or die, expressions of loss may arise naturally, and you can let them come and go of their own accord. Finally, you're free to be with others with a full and open heart. Love simply flowers as the fertile soil of all of life.

Only Celebration Remains

Every relationship, every interaction holds within it the seed of truth. Take a stand in freedom from mind-created projections, and a universe of potential opens up. The living reality of presence touches everything, from mundane conversations about routine details of everyday life to the most profound and pivotal interactions with people close to you. It takes less than a nanosecond to drop the veils that make you think you're separate, clearing the way for fearless and loving ways of being.

Start by realizing that before any person, thought, feeling, or situation, you are here, being, present and aware. And this awareness is at the heart of everything.

Presence transforms relationships, and the transformation begins with an honest self-appraisal. Tell yourself the truth about what you need, fear, and avoid, and how this affects your relationships. Examine your subtle strategies to control and acquire.

Right now, commit to no longer blaming others or expecting them to change. The source of peace is nowhere else but within you. In fact, when you let go of all conditioning, you realize it is you! The solution to the disappointment and frustration you experience in your relationships is more available, more possible, than the mind could ever imagine.

It takes no time at all, only the willingness to shed identities in the service of love. Use the pain of fear and lack as a signal to become very alert to your experience. Let

" Without your familiar habits, and their familiar, unfulfilling results, who are you?
You're spacious, open, here, whole, available, alive."

the urges to run, cling, and resist burn in the fire of awareness before you act. Lose interest in any comparing thoughts or misguided beliefs.

Without your familiar habits, and their familiar, unfulfilling results, who are you? You're spacious, open, here, whole, available, alive. Your relationships appear, always touched by love. The moments of interacting with "others" are experienced as an unending celebration of life itself.

Explorations

1. Uncover your beliefs about how relationships are supposed to be. Do you have ideas about how family members should treat each other? Do you expect your partner or friends to act in a certain way? How do these beliefs affect your relationships?

2. If your starting point were unity and love—not fear, need, or lack—reflect on how you would show up differently in your closest relationships.

3. Experiment with seeing familiar people—family members, co-workers, those who irritate you most—with fresh eyes. Pretend you're meeting them for the first time, with no history and no established patterns of relating. Let yourself be surprised by the insights you discover.

4. When you're triggered during an interaction, pause, be silent, and open to your experience instead of reacting or saying how you feel. Welcome whatever arises in you, as best you can.

5. What—and who—are you attached to? What do you think you need from your relationships so you can be happy? Return your attention to the simplicity of being aware. Notice that who you are is already whole and fulfilled.

Listen to the guided audio meditation at
www.GailBrenner.com/books.

9

Natural Curiosity

As you begin to know your true nature as aware presence, questions invariably arise. These questions emerge from a curious mind awakening from the trance of conditioning. This is a mind ready to look beyond habits to discover what it doesn't know. It's a beautiful mind, open like the sky.

Questions that arise are the mind's attempts to know something that it can't mentally understand. Minds work by studying objects to figure them out. But your true identity is not an object— it's the living experience of aware presence itself. You know it, not with your mind, but by consciously being what you already are. Questioning—and allowing answers to arise unforced—helps to soften the tendency to know by thinking. Rather than trying to find answers, you're receptive to the alive experience of you that is always here, outside of the thinking mind.

By its very functioning, the mind distorts and misunderstands. It creates beliefs *about* reality, but these have little bearing on the actual experience of what's real. No belief or idea can ever convey the true nature of reality. Like trying to describe

> "By its very functioning, the mind distorts and misunderstands. No belief or idea can ever convey the true nature of reality."

how an apple tastes to someone who's never eaten one, all descriptions fall short. How do you know the taste of an apple? You take a bite and experience the flavor first-hand. Likewise, the only way to know formless being, completely at peace with everything, is to experience it.

Questions invite you to investigate your beliefs. Maybe you believe that difficult feelings will never arise again once you're grounded in the awakened state. (Not true.) Or perhaps you believe the mind will always be quiet. (Also not true.) Recognize the belief, then move from "I know how it is" to not knowing. Be open to the in-the-moment unfolding of life unhindered by your ideas about it. Your direct experience of what's happening *is* the answer. And this is always available.

For most of us, the idea of being limited, separate individuals dies a slow death. The mind and body hold onto what's familiar, even if it invokes suffering. And separation is familiar. This fear-based way of being stays very much intact through resisting what's true—and through unquestioned acceptance or resignation. Beginning to question it is a very good sign.

So is applying what you hear to your direct experience in the moment. I remember exactly when the light bulb lit up for me and I stopped passively listening to teachings and waiting for divine intervention. I realized, with my whole being, that I was being invited to investigate my conditioning and realize the truth of what's always been here and always at peace. When my mind stopped trying to figure it all out, I realized I hadn't before been genuinely curious about looking deeply within. I now had faith that knowing the light of my true nature was possible for me.

What would it actually feel like to let a familiar habit fall away—just for a moment? What's the actual experience of an unexamined feeling, such as anger or shame? What if you and others are not separate entities, but illuminated by life itself—at one with the timeless now? These questions and their answers breed useful and revealing opportunities for clarity.

Here are some answers to common questions and misunderstandings that arise along the pathless path back to yourself. As you read them, bring them alive in you. Let yourself not know. Use your attention to explore the absolute truth in your experience. Be exquisitely open to abandoning the familiar habitual grooves of believing, thinking, and feeling. Release attention from the objects of conditioning and let it fall naturally into itself—revealing the direct knowing of the unity of all.

"What do you mean when you say that I'm not a separate self?"

Before this pointed investigation, if someone asked you who you are, you'd probably state your name, gender, age, personality characteristics, history, likes and dislikes. You might point to your body or a photograph of you and say, "This is me."

You might define yourself by your habits, roles, and tendencies. "I'm someone who needs a lot of attention and approval from others." "I'm independent and don't rely on people for anything." "I'm a loving wife and mother." "I'm a vice president in a large corporation." These labels and identities support the seemingly obvious conclusion that you are a unique individual.

The idea of you as a separate self creates an inside and outside, where you believe that you're here, and the world is out there—separate from you. Since most other people hold a similar belief, we think we live in a world populated by billions of separate selves. On one level, this is true. You do live in the world and function as a separate person. It seems so normal—until you start fearlessly asking questions.

Why even embark on this investigation? *Because believing yourself to be separate is unsatisfying.* It leaves you with the feeling that there must be more.

As you question the idea of you as a separate self, you make the amazing discovery that no such thing exists. You find that "the body" is only a set of sensations. When you close your eyes, where does the body go? You realize that the idea of you as a separate self needs thoughts to maintain itself. Who are you when you're not thinking about yourself, your past, and your future?

You grasp that everything about what you call 'you' is temporary, even ephemeral. It's all changeable, and it all depends on thinking. You're not who you thought you were. And if you aren't, neither are those other seemingly separate selves out there.

If your idea of yourself collapses as you investigate it, then who are you?

As you let all of these identifications and beliefs fall away, because they're not true, you realize that something remains— something awake and alive. It is you, pure being! Without the mind-created ideas of time and space, there is *This*, aware presence, with nothing in it. You've found the bare substance of reality, which can't be separate from itself. And because it only is itself, there's no conflict, no worrying, no trying to get or escape—no suffering, only life experienced everywhere.

If you believe yourself to be separate, you'll do your best to piece a life together. But if you discover that all your beliefs are false, what remains is you—alive, very well, and completely at peace—even with whatever uncomfortable sensations may be arising in the moment. This is the beginning of your true, full, human life that emerges from wholeness, not fear.

"I've heard that I need to stop my thoughts. Is that true?"

Pure being has no problem when thoughts appear—and they will appear. The idea that you should stop your thoughts and that your mind should be silent is a myth. If thoughts arise and you want to get rid of them, you're saying, "No," to what's actually here. Your attention has been taken in by thoughts admonishing you to banish your thoughts!

You're arguing with what's here, believing that something's wrong with things as they are. And you're refueling the mind's hope for the thoughts to be silenced. Meanwhile, with your attention on a supposed better future when your mind is finally quiet, you're missing the fullness of life, here right now. This is resistance to what is—and an opportunity for your attention to gently fall back into being.

Awareness is the backdrop to everything and its nature is pure peace with all that arises, including thoughts. This peaceful presence doesn't stand guard to your inner landscape, comparing experiences and finding thoughtlessness more acceptable than having thoughts appear. It doesn't say, "yes" to joyful experiences and "no" to troubling thoughts. If that's what is happening, your personal desires are at play, and the knowing of pure being has been forgotten in that moment.

The question about stopping thoughts arises if you're identifying as the you who views thinking as a problem. Maybe you're reacting to repetitive, compulsive thoughts that never seem to leave you alone. These are the ones that pervade your mind-space, keep you up at night, and feed stress and tension. You wish you could just find relief from them. Or maybe you believe that in order to know yourself as timeless, silent presence, you need to make thoughts disappear. Either way, you've gotten off-track if you're trying to stop them.

To stop your thoughts, you would need to notice them, somehow get rid of them, and make sure they don't reappear— while trying to remain peaceful and stress-free. All of this effort is unsustainable.

Rather than being a problem, the appearance of thoughts can be held as an opportunity. Isolate any thought that arises. The normal tendency would be to think about how you want this thought to evaporate and come up with strategies to make it disappear—which is only more thinking and more effort.

Instead, get curious beyond the content of the thought. Step back from it and inquire, "What is this thing called a thought? Where did it come from? Where does it go when it leaves?" Follow any thought back to its source, and you'll find pure awareness. It's the silent ground of being that is free of thought, yet is never disturbed when thoughts arise.

> *"Get curious beyond the content of the thought."*

The true solution to thinking is to realize that the one who thinks she needs to stop thoughts is also only a thought. Who are you? Are you your body or your thinking? These are temporary appearances that emerge from presence. Don't worry about any thoughts that arise, and know yourself as the substance of everything—formless, whole, alive, completely at peace.

Let your attention melt back into its source: loving presence. Then thoughts appearing are no different than a fleeting wisp of cloud in the evening sky. And when you understand that reality is timeless, there's no time for a thought—or even a word or sound—to form. Any concern about thoughts naturally falls away as attention rests in pure, silent being, undivided from itself.

"I don't like the way I am. I have bad habits that make me unhappy. Don't I need to improve or change myself?"

Personal unhappiness is often the spark that ignites the search for true and lasting peace. We all want to know how to be happy.

And it makes sense that we would try to improve what we don't like about ourselves and what isn't working in our lives.

But here's the problem. This approach of self-improvement feeds the idea of a better you that you hope to become at some future time. The wish to improve yourself assumes that you—and your current reality—aren't good enough. It contains the fundamental misunderstanding that you're a separate entity. And from this point of view, you'll never be fulfilled or satisfied.

This mindset of lack assumes that you're missing something that could make you whole, while ignoring your essential wholeness. It beckons you to imagine a better future, while locking you into believing that now isn't enough. If you think you need to improve, you're taking as true thoughts that compare, judge, plan, and hope. This is a convoluted web of thinking that keeps you searching—and it's the foundation of the whole self-help industry. It won't reveal the happiness you seek—because you're looking in the wrong place.

When feelings of personal lack arise along with the wish for a better future, recognize that patterns of thinking have taken hold. Don't get stuck in hoping and fixing. Experiment with letting all of these thoughts float off like a leaf in the wind. Recognize that without giving them meaning, you're here, already at peace. You don't need to move one millimeter to discover happiness.

You stop doing the impossible task of self-improvement and realize that you're already complete. It's such a relief to stop believing you're inadequate and need to be fixed. These beliefs drive so much suffering!

Then, from this place of fullness and clarity, maybe changes will happen—but not to fix the mythical separate self. It will become natural to adjust your life circumstances, begin expressing yourself without the limitation of fear, and show up openhearted in your relationships. You may notice that you consciously feel the drive behind compulsive habits as your behavior changes—or that you're ready to align your life choices with this knowing of who you are as the undivided whole.

And this is the irony: how you feel and how you function in life does improve—but it doesn't come from improving the illusory separate self. Allow your attention to rest in the ground of awareness from which all thoughts and feelings arise, and paradoxically, things improve on their own without the desperate trying of the personal self to be different. You might notice a simple, "Oh," as you find your way with ease to the perfect fit in any moment.

Knowing yourself as loving presence, there's no need to search, seek, find, or fix. As you give up these tendencies, you realize you've always been here, aware and alive. You've discovered the jewel in the lotus flower.

"How do I accept things as they are? I have trouble accepting myself, and I find certain situations unacceptable."

By its very nature, pure formless being cannot find anything unacceptable. It's the source of everything, with no exception. You can't move away from it because everything is you! This is unity, undivided consciousness, the absolute truth. When you're grounded as this awareness, the question of acceptance can't even arise.

Check it out in your own experience. Shift your attention to being aware of awareness. You might notice thought forms or physical sensations, but from this place of being aware, there's no problem with any of them—and no struggle about whether or not you're able to accept them. They're simply here.

The question about accepting things as they are comes from the mind and from the idea of you as a personal self needing to improve. From this perspective, you seem to have two choices: accept or resist. You can offer a welcoming, "Yes, this is how it is," or a rejecting, "No, I want this to be different." When you accept, you're aligned with the truth of reality, which is already accepting, and you're surrendering your personal desires to life as it appears. Resisting strengthens the idea of the limited self by fighting, avoiding, and denying what's here.

Acceptance is an enthusiastic embracing of what is. It isn't passive, and it won't resign you to wallowing forever in difficult emotions or barely tolerating your circumstances. It doesn't mean that your habits and life situation won't change or that you should condone hurtful and damaging behavior. And it certainly doesn't preclude you from saying, "No."

Acceptance—simple being—is only about receiving what is, as it is. It simply says, "Oh, this. This is how it is right now." It turns your attention away from the mind's activity of resistance to show you the truth in the moment. It takes you out of denial of your actual experience.

If you find yourself battling with what is, then your mind has enticed you into believing thoughts about how things should be different than they are. It convinces you that you should be thinner or more successful. It tells you that the stories you hear on the news shouldn't be happening or that you shouldn't have been passed over for that promotion.

Yes, unfair and incomprehensible things happen. And maybe you want to clean up your eating habits. But calling the way things actually are unacceptable feeds resistance, not peace. Not accepting creates an inner division that leaves you feeling frustrated, helpless, and conflicted. And if you live in these stories about how things should be different, you're diverting your attention from aware presence, here now and perfectly at peace. If you're interested in the deepest happiness, you'll want to investigate how your mind resists—and let it be as you fall into yourself, relishing peace.

Non-acceptance infiltrates so many everyday situations. You might first notice stress and discontent. Then you conclude that you had a rough day or that life isn't all it's cracked up to be. If you explore your direct experience, you'll find physical sensations that contract against what's happening.

What would it take to live in acceptance? You'd let go of *any beliefs* that pull your attention away from the bare experience of now. Without chewing on thoughts of should and shouldn't, what do you feel? What sensations are present in your body? From the field of awareness, meet them fully, and they'll no longer fuel agitating stories.

You may notice a sense of relief as you stop the effort of resisting and come into sync with things as they are. And you may become aware of uncomfortable feelings that you'd been avoiding through the mind activity of resistance—which sparks truthful investigation. This is the movement toward love, in love.

Once the veils of resistance are lifted, the stage is set for wise action. Resistance closes down creativity and causes the mind to spin. It keeps you from finding the best solutions or changing in the most efficient ways. But deeply accepting what's here taps into infinite possibilities revealed in perfect alignment with all that is.

"*I've tried doing what you suggest but it hasn't worked.*"

This statement is the product of a mind that compares, expects, and imagines. It doesn't mean that you're not trying hard enough or that you're not doing it right. It suggests that you have an idea about how happiness looks and feels that doesn't match your current experience. And it speaks to a relationship between objects in time: "If I do what you suggest then I should be at peace." None of this expresses the true nature of reality.

Yes, of course you want to feel better. But thoughts like these keep your mind engaged, while you overlook the peaceful, aware presence that's always here, at the heart of everything. Imagining what awakening is like and how your life should be when this realization happens are simply thoughts that appear in the infinite space of who you are. A simple shift of attention to the experience of being aware will reveal all that you're looking for.

> "*Imagining what awakening is like and how your life should be when this realization happens are simply thoughts that appear in the infinite space of who you are.*"

Throughout this book, I've offered suggestions for tools and practices that can support the discovery of who you are. For example, you might consciously reflect on thoughts and feelings that make up a habit, so you can be more aware when the habit takes hold. Or you might intentionally shift your attention away from thinking to your body and to awareness itself. These suggestions aren't about changing you, because there's no "you" to change. They're only to point to what you've overlooked—pure peace, the substance of this now moment, which is always available to know in your conscious experience.

Aware presence just is, and it is here endlessly. It doesn't worry about whether happiness will last or whether, in the next moment, you'll be stuck or free. And it doesn't mind that stressful thoughts or feelings continue to appear. These concerns are signs that your mind is in charge. Presence has always been full and complete within itself—and at peace with whatever arises in it. It's only interested in freedom now—because only now exists.

Does a practice "work?" It's the mind that stands back and judges your experience.

Yet, it often takes time to unwind conditioning. It *will* reappear and grab you—maybe often, in the beginning. But it doesn't matter how many times a reactive pattern arises because every time is an opportunity to know yourself as peace. Orient your whole life toward freedom in every way possible. Your fire for it burns up the force of habitual ways of being, each time yielding to ease and space. Eventually, you'll experience the slightest nudge to pick up a pattern, and you'll have enough awareness to stay rooted as peace.

"Okay, it's the mind that judges whether a practice works. But are practices useful?"

Yes, practices can be useful for a time. Or you might continue them simply out of enjoyment. It might be helpful to take time to sit quietly and simply be, which is what we commonly call meditation. This practice invites you into the possibility of resting in your true nature as infinite peace. It supports you to disconnect from familiar, chronic mental and emotional habits that have come to define you.

Meditation involves simply being aware in the timeless flow of experiencing. You notice hearing, feeling, sensing, all arising in and inseparable from being. You realize that you can disengage from the stories in your mind and stay as awareness as you experience the urge to act. You can fully and lovingly welcome your feelings. Eventually, you realize that meditation isn't something you do; it's effortlessly being who you are.

Consciously practicing being with what is has been extremely helpful in my journey. Once I understood the make-up of conditioned habits, I stopped resisting any reaction. Every single time I felt the twinge of an emotion, I sat on my sofa and shifted to a completely accepting space for it to move through without the complication of any story. Over and over, intense feelings arose, primarily in the form of physical sensations, and I said, "Yes!" to each and every one of them with no hesitation whatsoever.

There was no goal, no doing—I simply allowed what was happening to happen. I literally felt inner walls collapsing as everything was welcomed in from the shadows of my mind and body. Needless to say, I spent a lot of time on the sofa! And over time I noticed an effortless release of habits. I was already light and happy before my mind started realizing it.

When it comes to happiness and freedom, do what you feel drawn to and what you enjoy. You might read spiritual books that support awakening, attend retreats, or meet others with similar interests. Quieting practices like gentle yoga, mindful walks in nature, and consciously being aware presence in daily life help to focus your attention on this now moment. And you might get out there into the world, following your passion and enthusiasm without reservation.

Consciously stop taking anything for granted and know that you're full and alive. Turn your attention away from being stuck in mental and emotional turmoil, and see everyone and everything with fresh eyes and an open heart. Recognize gratitude, amazement, and wonder, playing with the possibility that everything is you—and it is!

Even a few moments of meeting things as they truly are offers a glimpse into your true nature.

When it comes to practices, be aware of this paradox. On the surface, it looks like you're applying strategies or techniques that make you happier. But actually, you're consciously knowing who you are more often. Although it may seem like you're becoming more peaceful or that your troubles are disappearing, you aren't going anywhere or becoming anything. Your path is much more radical than that—it's about ending the belief that you're separate. You realize you've always been peaceful and aware. This isn't a place and it's not somewhere else. It's here, now, the timeless presence of being.

Let these practices do their work. Let them melt your separate identity and show you that you already are the happiness you seek. You might dissolve into an endlessly opening heart, bathe in the perfume of experiencing the unity of all, be awestruck by the seemingly mundane and ordinary aspects of daily life. And you might notice nothing—but wake up one day to realize that you're truly peaceful and happy.

Practices contain an element of doing. Eventually, they no longer need to be done—and you continue them, or not. I've watched my mind tell me I should meditate more while I'm happily enjoying my interactions with the world in all its forms. Who is it who thought I needed to meditate? In choosing practices—or not to practice—don't let thoughts be your guide. Listen to the truth as it expresses itself through you. Tap into what you really want, and let your natural intelligence steer you. You may practice, as the Buddha said, like your hair is on fire. Or you may rest in effortless contentment—or anywhere in between. In the end, it doesn't really matter. You're here, full and complete, reflected everywhere.

"You talk a lot about the body and physical sensations. Why are they so important?"

Sensations in the body are an important gateway to knowing your true nature. When we're on automatic, our habits and tendencies run outside of conscious awareness. And often we find ourselves caught in thinking—ruminating, worrying, and trying to figure it all out. We're barely aware of just a piece of the totality of our experience.

We've seen that when we shine the light of awareness on what's actually happening, we notice stories we tell ourselves in our minds and physical sensations, all appearing in aware presence. The stories are a collection of thoughts *about* what's happening and will never reveal the deepest peace. You need to look outside the mind to your direct experience to discover who you are.

Often ignored, sensations in the body are the first sign that a conditioned habit is emerging. Whatever derails your happiness—a desire to seek approval, incessant complaining, out-of-control emotions—if you trace your experience back to its source, you'll find a physical contraction. But excessive thinking, feeling, and behaving divert you from this knowing.

Become familiar with the structure of habits so you can notice the sensations that underlie them. Then you can relax into aware being, creating an open and loving space to allow the sensations to be. You're not attached to whether or not they're present and you're not ignoring them because they're uncomfortable. This is the sacred practice that lets the mental and emotional habits unwind.

As humans in bodies, physical sensation is our first reaction to people and events in our environment. When we were infants, we didn't have the mental capacity to think, but we could certainly feel sensation. When our needs were met and we felt safe and cared for, the body could stay relaxed. But any threat to safety caused it to contract.

For most of us, these contractions pile up because they were unexplored and unresolved. And as we get older, compulsive thinking comes into play—offering a useful mechanism that avoids all this uncomfortable feeling.

But when you notice physical sensation without resisting it, you discover that, in and of itself, it has no meaning whatsoever. What is sensation? Nothing—unless you label it and make a story out of it. What could be more freeing?

When you begin to pay attention to physical sensations, a whole world may open up to you. Some people have been numb to their bodies, not even realizing they were experiencing sensations. Others may feel blocks of sensation that they have been avoiding for a very long time. With the desire for true happiness, you finally welcome these congealed and unexplored sensations into presence. Without giving them meaning through a story, in the moment they're welcomed they release their grip.

In reality, there is no thing called the body. If you close your eyes and sense whatever's present, you'll know that the body only seems to exist if you see and label it. There's really just sensation appearing in presence.

As you experience sensations from the perspective of conscious awareness, you understand what they actually are—arisings in the moment that mean nothing and have no power. And when we know consciousness as timeless, even to say they arise isn't correct. There is no time for arising. There's only the timeless now, so incredibly still.

Notice the physical sensations without attaching any story. Then be the awareness that sensation arises in. Lose the capacity for thought and language, and know that you're free.

"I'm waiting to have an epiphany. Isn't that what needs to happen?"

If you hang around in the world of spirituality long enough, you'll come up with all kinds of ideas about what needs to happen in order to know yourself as aware presence. You'll tell yourself you need to have an epiphany…or see the light…or go to five retreats a year…or meditate an hour a day.

These lovely imaginings of a curious mind have nothing to do with reality. In fact, they feed the belief that some event needs to happen so you can realize who you are. And they overlook the ever-present now, existing right here before the mind takes hold.

You don't need to experience an epiphany or any other special occurrence to know the truth of your being. You're living it right now—although the mind may not realize it—because it can't be any other way. You are, right now in this moment, exactly what you're searching for—undivided consciousness, infinite formless presence totally at peace with itself.

> " You don't need to experience an epiphany or any other special occurrence to know the truth of your being. You're living it right now— although the mind may not realize it— because it can't be any other way."

If you're waiting for some grand understanding to arrive in your awareness, what you really want is to consciously know what is already your reality. You won't find it if you're looking for an experience that may happen in the future or if you try to reason your way to the realization.

The place to look is outside the mind, not within it. And the way to look there is directly into the bare experience of now. This means looking at that which is looking—the pure experience of being aware. There's no "you" trying to find an object that is reality. If you're looking for something you think isn't here yet, you've let the mind re-create the idea of time and entice you into thinking you might find it in the future. And you've turned boundless life that includes everything into division—you and an object you're searching for. Take this as a signal to stop. See all beliefs as false, and they'll collapse in a heap. Experience the utter sweetness that remains.

Notice how you don't need anything—no epiphany or special experience—to discover what's already here. You're already it!

And in the vastness of you, fantastic experiences sometimes occur. You might dissolve into bliss or oneness. You might experience the pure vibration of life. You might feel love meeting itself everywhere with unimaginable intimacy. These experiences contain an element of truth, but if they come and go, they, too, are temporary appearances that arise in awareness. If you grab onto them and want them to return when they're gone, your mind has created a separate you who is at odds with the flow of life. And you've attached to an idea about how reality is supposed to be.

The end of suffering is not an experience—it's realizing that, at the core, everything is you. You're not limited by beliefs and emotions—you're everywhere, overflowing with infinite potential. If a vivid experience visits you, don't try to get back to it once it subsides. Simply let it go, bathe in its perfume, and be here now. What you want to discover is everywhere—even right here in the midst of ordinary daily life.

Let yourself expand into who you've always been beyond all beliefs. You already are the treasure you seek.

Many more questions may arise as you contemplate the nature of reality. Find the true question, and ask it without knowing or expecting anything. Then listen, not to the mind, but to the light of truth, where all questions are answered. If you do one thing, follow joy and be happy now.

Explorations

1. Reflect on the questions that come up in your mind. Do they deepen your understanding and direct experience of the truth—or do they cause your mind to spin?

2. A question implies that you don't know the answer. Can you not know and let the answers come?

3. How can you more completely say Yes! to your experience—to life as it appears to you?

Listen to the guided audio meditation at
www.GailBrenner.com/books.

10

Finally Home

By now, you might be wondering what it's like to live free of the trap of believing you're a separate, limited self. Well, you're already doing just that. The current of life continuously unfolds as the ever-present, timeless now. It is bursting with potential to express itself in an infinite number of ways. You breathe, move, hear, speak. Your body is functioning, which is miraculous in itself. Whether or not you're caught in the prison of separation, life is happening quite naturally.

It's obvious—and amazing! Once you realize you don't need the sense of the personal self to live—you don't need to protect or defend yourself—you're free to allow the most natural responses to emerge from you. And they'll be way more heartfelt and appropriate than responses based on fear or need. You realize that no hole exists inside you—that you're not somehow damaged or insufficient—and you no longer feel compelled to:

- Present yourself in a positive light;

- Keep yourself safe;

> *"Once you realize you don't need the sense of the personal self to live—you don't need to protect or defend yourself—you're free to allow the most natural responses to emerge from you."*

- Be right;

- Worry about making mistakes.

You don't need to keep control. Yet, you show up fully alive, available to what's happening, receptive and alert. And everything is just fine.

As you consciously live in this unfolding, you experience your body and mind as part of the totality. You no longer need to serve the personal self—with its need to improve. Not only do you "go with the flow," you literally *are* the flow. Life is; it simply happens. And it is absolutely possible to live this way in the world, both engaged and unattached.

When old thought patterns, emotions, and tendencies arise—and they will—don't avoid or indulge them. You know that these conditioned reactions are illusory forms arising in consciousness. But recognize them, feel them, and realize what's absolutely true in your experience. Use each of these moments to re-discover presence and peace.

In the areas where you're still identified with the mind, your experience will be sticky:

- Am I meeting my goals?

- My plans didn't work out.

- My relationships are unsatisfying.

- I can't find my life purpose.

- I'm not happy.

- My habits keep overtaking me.

If thoughts like these define you, you'll be confused and troubled.

As you recognize the purity of being and surrender to love, peace, and happiness, life will naturally simplify, and you'll read the rest of this chapter to celebrate what you already know. But if you're in the ongoing process of dis-identifying with the personal self, bring a laser-like inquiry to what you're experiencing so you can discover what's true.

Flexible Being

The conditioned mind is inflexible and repetitive. Once it arrives in a comfort zone where it thinks it knows what to do, creative responses disappear and you go on automatic, playing out habits time after time. It's like being half-dead.

A friend was relating about her well-entrenched tendency to try to fix problems. Her mind is very adept at seeing exactly what others should do so that they are happier, healthier, and better adjusted, and she tirelessly offers these ideas (to mixed reviews). This habit of fixing automatically takes over, making her unable to discover her own best response in a given situation.

I suggested that this tendency was a habit and invited her to refrain from showing interest in it. This opened up a world of possibility! She realized she could listen, empathize, do nothing, reflect on the urges and feelings that arise in her, or do anything else that meets the situation as it is, rather than as her mind interprets it. The veil of the habit began to fall away.

As you release each habit and identification, you're more consciously aligned with the undivided fullness of you. Free of identification, the mind is infinitely flexible. You're available to the freshness of the moment—and that opens possibilities unconditioned by habit or expectation, by past or future.

The sensitivity to suffering becomes more and more finely honed. What seemed normal before may feel intensely painful—but that pain awakens you. Behaviors like killing an insect, speaking harshly to yourself or someone else, gossiping, or behaving dishonestly no longer feel normal. You just can't respond in the same way anymore—so you're surprised by the spontaneous response that occurs in the moment. You lose the capacity to perceive things as separate—and that changes everything.

Acting as if you are who you actually are may be just what you need to break down the mind's rigidity. Try acting as if you're whole, free of pain from your past, bigger than your imagined limits. See through the eyes of non-division, where everything is you. These experiments challenge the habits and ingrained belief systems that create the illusion of separation and offer a glimpse into living as everyday presence.

Finding Fearlessness

Living this understanding isn't spiritual or otherworldly. It's real, visceral, and directly applicable to your life experience. Instead of sleepwalking, you're alive in your life, more fully human than ever before. Even brief connections are intimate. Decisions come with so much ease and clarity that they don't feel like decisions at all. A mind uncluttered by repetitive thought doesn't need to control or protect—so living fearlessly in the unknown is the way of life.

This might sound attractive, but how do you give up control and live fearlessly? By recognizing the fear-based "need" to control and realizing that it doesn't define you. Without changing or getting rid of anything, you embrace the way these tendencies appear in the moment. Then clear seeing invites the mind to naturally return to its source as aware presence. And a mind awake to itself is completely at rest, not agitated by thoughts.

Over time, without the veil of the separate self, it's natural to turn your attention from mental chatter and personal needs to pure presence. Confusion subsides as you learn to trust that this now moment offers everything you need to function seamlessly, in undisturbed peace. You know reality as completely safe—not from the perspective of the personal self, but from understanding the perfection of everything just as it is.

You're no longer willing to tolerate your own dissatisfaction and unhappiness. You become motivated to discover that peace lies at the heart of your conditioned patterns. And you enjoy this discovery time after time. You do what you know in your heart is true for you, even if you experience fear—which you know as only a fleeting physical sensation. You become impervious to others' approval or disapproval—it simply doesn't land anymore because there's no separate you for it to land on. Clarity shows you how to clean up your relationships and your long-unaddressed life circumstances. And you're free to enjoy, appreciate, love, savor, and revel in the immediacy of now.

Seeing Through Stress

If you experience stress, you're allowing thoughts to guide your life. I don't mean the fight-or-flight response that makes you run from physical danger, the feeling you experience from a challenging and enjoyable activity like rock climbing, or the extra load on your heart when you exercise. These aren't problematic forms of stress.

But what happens when you're chronically filled with thoughts about too much to do and not enough time to do it? You've created a mental idea of how things should be which pulls your attention away from presence. And you feel anxiety, agitation, and pressure.

I sometimes become aware that I've been running from one thing to another with a sense of urgency that's not real. A moment of investigation reveals that I've gotten attached to thoughts about all the things that need to be done, believing them to be true. This is the golden opportunity to let attention release from them and effortlessly return to awareness and ease.

If you let go of your beliefs about what *has* to be done, you'll do exactly what *needs* to be done. For many of us who are over-committed, seemingly important tasks may fall away—because you understand that the motivation behind doing them is false and stressful.

So where does motivation come from? Surrender your personal beliefs and desires, and the natural intelligence of presence will guide you. Know that you are already one with life, and you'll be moved from the undivided whole and not from fear. The wholeness of life will show you where you're still caught in conditioning, inviting you to meet your experience lovingly and return to peace.

You can trust that you'll have just what you need. Maybe not as much as your mind says you need or in the way you want it, but what appears will be a perfect expression of life in form. Why? Because that's what's here. Once you no longer pay attention to insistent, incessant thoughts telling you to be more, do more, and have more, you realize that things are just fine as they are—and so are you!

The Sensitive Body

As we've discovered, habits lie lodged in the physical body as contraction, tension, and holding. Even though you can cut through the mental story of the habit, the physical aspect still takes time to release. Some patterns may have been held in the body for a very long time with no attention paid to them. Once you stop identifying with them as components of the personal self, you know them as just physical sensations. And that gives them the space to unwind—down to the cellular level and beyond.

You may experience strong releases of energy, or the changes may be subtle. Keeping your attention rooted in presence, with no expectation about what should or shouldn't happen, the body will realign naturally over time.

Experience in the physical body serves as an interface with the world. The first moment of identifying as separate begins with an overlooked physical contraction. As your attention rests as awareness, you're alert to these subtle sensations. If they go unnoticed, a story spins its enticing trap—and you'll wake up to realize that you've been captured by thought and emotion. But acknowledge them as they arise, and you—awareness—remain undisturbed.

Someone in your household does something that irritates you, and you start down the road to feeling hurt or disappointed. You lash out in anger or reach for a glass of wine. This is where the spiritual rubber meets the road in everyday life. You can let these habits take you away, or you can stay present as presence. And your attention will show you that each habit starts with a physical sensation—a contraction that says, "No!" to your experience in the moment.

Recognize this physical "No!"—and peace becomes possible. You experience the truth without the overlay of the story. You may even feel like you're burning in sensation. But if you don't touch it with your attention, and you definitely don't feed the story about it, you know it as a temporary arising in the ocean of you. As you remember the essence of who you are, the habit, the story, the identification, even the discomfort of physical sensations—all of it collapses in a heap, and reality shines, completely at peace with itself.

For some time, most of us experience the dance of being caught by patterns then waking up to the truth of timeless presence. You believe you are a separate entity, then all division falls away to reveal the glorious now. You suffer by resisting, and then you pick up the breadcrumbs to return to your natural state. Each time you recognize a habit, the grip of conditioning softens. And each moment of recognition is a conscious return to timeless peace.

> *"Each time you recognize a habit, the grip of conditioning softens. And each moment of recognition is a conscious return to timeless peace."*

Awareness of physical sensation supports the release from identification. When you sit quietly, allow sensations to come and go. Invite contractions to be experienced, rather than hidden. Release the perceived edges of the body into space.

Don't try to make any experience change or go away; this feeds resistance, not peace. It's not that being aware "works" when you no longer feel uncomfortable sensations—and doesn't "work" if sensations are present. A goal of not experiencing a given sensation contains the false belief that the idea of the future will be better than the reality of now. Take away all the mental activity about what should and shouldn't be present—along with any concept of a future time—and here you are, in the direct experience of presence where there can't possibly be resistance to things as they are.

If you notice but don't resist physical sensation, if you allow it to just be, with no story (not even the story of you as a separate self—who is never truly at ease anyway), there's no problem whatsoever. Isn't this the peace you are trying so hard to search for? It's right here.

Not Mind-Driven

Living as who you are, not as who you take yourself to be, means not being directed by the mind. How can that be—not to use thoughts to direct the activities of your life? What about goals, plans, and tasks? The mind tells you that if you don't think, nothing will get done.

When you release your attachment to thoughts, you realize that life's occurrences are already guided by a natural intelligence that effortlessly knows what's required. Sure, mental habits can interfere—creating stress, confusion, and unhappiness. But when you lose interest in these thought patterns, you align consciously with the unfolding that's already here.

Without the turmoil of unnecessary thinking, you're clear, and life feels spacious and simple. Thoughts are tools rather than weapons or distractions, and you can trust that the ones you need will arise. You feel the movement toward wanting peaceful surroundings, and thoughts arise about how to organize the clutter on your desk. An idea for a creative project comes through, and thoughts help you figure out how to go about it. These practical thoughts appear, but the complications from a convoluted mind are gone.

Most repetitive thinking resists what's actually here. You may be shocked to realize how much you argue with reality. The way to discover this is by noticing your thoughts for a day or two. "He shouldn't have left his clothes on the floor." "She should call me when she knows she'll be late." "Why didn't he let me know he couldn't complete the project on time?" "If only I were earning more money." And we don't just think these thoughts once—they recycle endlessly in the mind, keeping us locked away from presence, taking up precious space and time.

These commonplace thoughts are accompanied by a physical contraction—an "Oh, no, this shouldn't be happening," an armoring against the world that feeds a story of suffering. When you are in this body-mind whirlwind, you're identified as separate, and you aren't relaxed and open. You're resisting, believing there's something wrong that needs to be fixed. It seems subtle until you realize how much it contributes to your overall discontent and prevents you from actually solving problems.

The end of the mind-driven life is the end of resistance. Resting in the now turns "Oh, no" into "Oh, this." You shift to a deep acceptance that eliminates extra thinking and allows space to respond effortlessly. If you don't want the clothes on the floor, you pick them up. If the project is late, you take the next needed step. Most importantly, you stop engaging with thoughts that make you believe there's something wrong with now. Instead, you effortlessly return to the palpable experience of aliveness that permeates everywhere. You're amazed at how drama subsides.

Everyday Life Circumstances

As clarity touches you, you may become aware of how strongly fear and lack have guided your decisions. Maybe you've stayed in an unsatisfying job because you fear a new or risky direction. Or perhaps you've avoided opening yourself to a relationship even though you long to. Or you prevented yourself from acting on creative impulses that you yearn to express.

You might be overcome by realizing how you've limited yourself through unconscious patterns based on false identities. I know I was, once understanding flooded in. But once you see the truth, you've opened the door to so many new opportunities.

Presence is here—even while the mind regrets past choices and bemoans what should and shouldn't have happened. Shift your attention here, and there's only *This*, eternally alive and new. It's never too late or too soon; there are no missed chances. You *are* this timeless presence. When you know this consciously, the mind-driven life is gone, and real life begins—now and now and now…

This realization may or may not lead to practical changes. For some people, this upheaval in consciousness takes time to settle—affecting relationships, jobs, living situation, and your daily activities. Roles that you took so seriously turn out to be transparent. You may show up differently to people who know you well—your partner, children, parents, friends—as you're now steeped in the integrity of clarity and full openheartedness. You no longer strategize to get or to defend. Stopping the dance that occurs in relationships can be unsettling—or relieving—to others.

For me, some friendships disappeared. My relationship with my parents improved tremendously. I married my life partner. And I spend much more time alone. The structure of my work as a psychotherapist has become less prominent, although the work—if you can call it that—flows as presence itself, offering complete trust in the moment-to-moment unfolding and unshakeable confidence in the healing power of knowing who you are. I'm happy, patient, and almost always fully open to what is.

My life looks "normal." I walk the dog, watch movies, enjoy yoga and other vigorous exercise, visit with friends, and appreciate the time I spend with my partner. I sit in formal meditation—for seconds or minutes—whenever I'm moved to (typically several times throughout the day and night). I'm not disturbed by the frustrations of daily life when things don't go as expected.

My commitment to truth is fierce. When conditioned patterns arise, they're never ignored. I immediately lose trust in the story, which reveals space for the breath, sensations, and whatever energy might be present. The return home starts out with intention and gives way to silent, effortless being.

It takes time to integrate everyday living with the realization of your true nature, and there's no endpoint as the realization touches all aspects of your life. Insights appear as you meet familiar situations with fresh eyes and a free heart. Resistance subsides, and deep contentment and peace reign.

Doing, Trying, and the Truth About Goals

The everyday living experience of presence is about being unified with the natural unfolding of life. Whatever happens simply emerges—unconditioned, uncaused, free. Appearing and disappearing happen instantaneously in the timeless now. From the point of view of the mind, it might sound like a wild ride.

How will you accomplish anything if you don't set goals? Don't you need to plan? What about your dreams and manifesting the life you want? If all is surrendered to presence, what then?

If you acknowledge all of these questions as mere thought forms with no inherent meaning, you realize that you're still here and alive. Does a separate entity need to exist for things to happen? Take away the idea of the one who needs to control, decide, and do—and find the natural, effortless unfolding. You can trust it completely, because it is reality itself. The personal self may take credit for what happens, thinking it has had a hand in controlling the outcomes that occur—but this is a misunderstanding.

Creating, doing, thinking, and achieving happen, but no separate entity creates, does, thinks, or achieves. If a thought appears about doing something to produce a certain outcome in the future, investigate it. Be curious about the motivation behind it. Does it come from fear, inadequacy, or need? Is there a hidden "should"? Do you believe that the outcome will make you into a better, happier, or more successful person? Or is it a pure expression of love?

An idea that derives from the separate self is fraught with trouble.

- It assumes there's a personal self responsible for the out-come—who can fail if the outcome doesn't occur.

- It contains the belief that happiness is attainable in the future—the dreaded "if only" way of thinking.

- It overlooks the possibility of the deepest happiness available now.

For a moment, abandon the belief in the separate self. An idea floats in that feels light and full of possibility. You envision the outcome, but you aren't attached to it. Whether the goal is accomplished or not means nothing for your self-worth or happiness. It's an impersonal idea, emerging from being that is already whole and infinitely happy.

"I'd like to write a book." "I need to figure out how to earn more money." "I want to get a promotion within a year." "I want to travel to India." "I'd like to learn to speak French." "I want a partner."

Any of these ideas can come from fear, lack, and inadequacy—or they can appear as a simple expression of the joy of being alive. When the illusion of the separate self disintegrates, the angst about accomplishing falls away. Without the self-doubt and pressure to prove yourself, doing arises from being. No longer muddled by personal insecurity and the need for others to approve of or admire you, you act humbly. You might work hard to achieve these goals, but your actions are clear and free of residue.

Do you procrastinate? Do you have a pattern of dropping projects before they're completed? It might be easy to rationalize: "Oh, I don't feel like doing that task right now. This is my present moment experience." Or you find yourself distracted by a myriad of other activities while you feed a cycle of regret and poor self-image.

If these thoughts are painful, they require investigation. You'll find that you've been avoiding the sensations of fear. As these go undetected, an identity as incapable or undeserving builds, and that stymies the creative flow. Realize that none of these objects is you—and the problem disappears.

On the other hand, maybe you're a doer, feeling pressured to meet goals or make a difference in the world. Are you on a personal mission? Are you strategizing to get a certain result to boost your self-esteem? These, again, are clues to identification as a separate person. Ultimately, they, too, keep you from realizing that you're already whole and happy in this very moment.

The everyday implications of this understanding about doing and goals are huge.

You're out of the way, and being takes over. Who knows what that will look like? You may be fired up to move mountains. Or you might sit on a bench for a year or two in bliss. Whatever path unfolds for you is natural—minus the shoulds and have-tos of the personal self.

The struggle over procrastination ends, with your attention fully in the now. You simplify the activities of your daily life, solve problems more effectively, and have the space to live in so much appreciation that your mind won't be able to take it in.

Be alert for happiness in your daily life—it may very well be there even if the mind hasn't realized it yet. Bring enthusiasm to the actions you take in the moments of life unfolding. Whatever you do, do it fully. Experience it. Enjoy it. Notice that beneath the resistance of the mind, peace is already here. It's an endless, everyday miracle.

> "*Be alert for happiness in your daily life it may very well be there even if the mind hasn't realized it yet.*"

What Is Your Life Purpose?

Much has been written about life purpose and personal fulfillment. Bookstores are loaded with books claiming to help you find your passion, the calling that will finally give your life meaning. For many—and I was one of them—this aspiration leaves you frustrated and lacking. It places you smack in the middle of the "if only" trap, delaying your happiness until you achieve an imagined better future.

The search for your life purpose assumes that you can find something you don't already have that will set everything right. It contains the belief that the present is incomplete, but could be fulfilled once the perfect activity becomes obvious. When you lean into how it makes you feel, you notice lack, hopelessness, and desperation. As you wonder who you are without a life purpose, you're bound to feel limited and small.

Thoughts about the future, a feeling of lack, ideas about personal fulfillment, comparing yourself to others who seem to have found happiness—these are all signs of the separate self. Your attention has become entangled with these thoughts and feelings that seem so true. If this is your reality, you've temporarily forgotten who you are.

Instead of accepting the thoughts as real, turn away from them. Deconstruct the feelings, and allow the physical sensations to be. You're not someone who needs to discover a fulfilling passion. You are loving, aware presence that's already fulfilled and eternally at peace.

This understanding makes your purpose easy to find: your purpose is one with whatever is happening now. What should you be doing? Exactly what you're doing now. Doing that comes from confusion about who you are will never feel satisfying because it's rooted in fear and propelled by a sense of inadequacy. But, as we've seen, doing that comes from being grounded in awareness is free and unconditioned. It has no agenda; it's a delightful expression of life overflowing.

Where is the need for a purpose? Without thoughts and feelings that congeal into a separate identity, there's no self and no problem. "Why haven't I succeeded? What should I be doing? What am I missing?" Questions that appear are seen as transparent experiences arising in awareness. If you don't touch them, they dissolve back into their source without disturbing you—and the entire life-purpose conundrum unravels.

If you're suffering because you don't know your purpose, there's only one thing to do. Instead of believing you're the one who needs to know it and going on a wild goose chase to find it, remember who you are—and you'll be liberated.

You'll find exactly what you thought you were missing. It's been here all along—you: boundless, exquisitely fresh, unendingly fulfilled.

Explorations

1. Enter a familiar situation as if you're not a separate entity. Let go of being mind-driven, and let love lead. Recognize that you're inseparable from everyone and everything. Watch as life unfolds perfectly.

2. Notice that trying and effort are products of the separate self. Put forth no effort whatsoever as you melt into presence. Simply let things happen.

3. Contemplate this: You're living your life purpose as the moments of your life unfold. It's no more complicated than that.

Listen to the guided audio meditation at
www.GailBrenner.com/books.

Acknowledgments

I'm grateful to those who have lit up the way for me with their teachings: Eli Jaxon-Bear, Gangaji, Rupert Spira, and Eckhart Tolle. And to those who have helped this book come to fruition: Shel Horowitz, Laurel Airica, and Wendy Newman.

With deepest love and appreciation for my partner, Cameron McColl, who has been a sounding board, guide, and all-around huge support during the birth of this book. He unendingly inspires me with the openness he brings to our relationship and his steadfast love of Truth.

To learn more, please visit www.GailBrenner.com